Read this first

This first part of the book almost always goes unread, what with students being so eager to get right to the work. We'll try not to delay you. However, you need to know a couple of things before starting. So that's why we have a large headline on this page.

First, this workbook works best as a companion to *Editing in the Electronic Era*, a marvelous textbook. They do not have to go together, but I hope they do. And I hope they get used all over the country. That happy circumstance, in addition to enriching the authors, produces some problems. For instance, a reference to the governor will have the name wrong in 49 states. Not only that, but the governor may lose the next election, leaving us with the wrong name in all 50.

Nettlesome.

Your workbook authors solved this one by using a real name, that of Bill Clements, governor of Texas. That happens to be the state where we live, and it's one of those we knew we could spell right. Most of the time we refer to "the governor" or "the mayor" or even "the president." You recognize this name problem and can handle it, no doubt. We're sorry we cannot tailor a workbook to every city. Our city, incidentally, is named Brightsville. A great place. It's the opposite of Dullsville.

Most of the exercises in this book have a generic approach--they can be used anywhere. Oh, you may have to do extra work if your local representatives are called aldermen instead of councilmen or council members. You can handle that, too.

* * *

Although colleges usually teach copy editing as preparation for work on a newspaper desk, we are aware that most of you will not spend your life in that pursuit. We have some newspaper orientation here, dealing mainly in news stories instead of publicity releases. But we have prepared the material to teach you to deal with the kinds of problems you will run into in all kinds of writing and editing.

Indeed, you can make an argument that writing and editing are part of the same process. If you learn to improve your own writing in this course, you will have made a good trade for your time.

The stories in this book generally come from real life. We have had to adjust a few because we want them to reflect real problems. Some stories will have more mistakes than would be acceptable in a reporter's copy. We overloaded some of those rather than looking around for a separate story to illustrate every writing flaw.

We also hope to help you develop a new kind of mind-set as you go through copy. We want you to read for understanding, reading as someone unfamiliar with the story would read. As a copy editor, you must help get ideas out of a writer's head into the reader's with no loss of understanding. So you have to see things from two perspectives.

Good copy editors make sure the commas are in the right places and get all the spelling and syntax right. They check names in the city directory (at the end of this book). They also keep their manure detectors turned on, and they cry out when some piece of nonsense comes across their video display tube. You may even detect a little of that in some of these exercises. Good luck.

Editing in the Electronic Era

WORKBOOK

by Martin L. Gibson
and L. Dupre Long

Iowa State University Press, Ames

Martin L. Gibson is Regents Professor of Communication, University of Texas at Austin.
L. Dupre Long is a lecturer in the Department of Journalism, University of Texas at Austin.

© 1987 Iowa State University Press, Ames, Iowa 50010
All rights reserved

Manufactured in the United States of America
♾ This book is printed on acid-free paper.

First edition, 1987
Second printing, 1990
Third printing, 1992

International Standard Book Number: 0-8138-0966-5

Contents

Read this first, v

Symbols, 1

Style, 4

Grammar, 17

Syntax, 37

Spelling, 50

Attribution, 52

Quotation, 77

Clutter, 87

Libel and ethics, 93

A word on math, 105

Editing, 108

Headlines, 154

Brightsville Directory, 169

Symbols

Your name _____

Date _____

Symbols — the basics

This is not an editing exercise. Do not delete material unless instructed to do so, regardless of seeming irrelevancies. This work tests your ability to use proper editing marks, as considered in Chapter 3 of your textbook.

Mark this sentence to begin a paragraph.

Make this sentence part of the preceding paragraph.

Mark this paragraph properly. be sure to Capitalize Everything the right way including

Atlantic ocean. put in any ommited letters and tke out unnnecessary ones.

Joe said "Hi, Bill, say aren't you from Waynesboro Tenn? I was told you left April 21

1987 for Missoula Mont. I will be there on August 9-10."

(Insert your name after *gave:*) She gave a Popsicle.

Insert al mising leters and tak out all extrras.

(Replace these commas with dashes:) Many, some say all, oppose the plan.

(Delete the second and third words:) Many of the players showed up early.

This week end, some single women and tom boys will participate.

Separate wordsaccidentally typedtogether. Transpose misplacde lettres.

He lived on cisco St. in some town in Calif. and he had eleven dogs and 9 cats.

(Fix it all, including style:) The companies coudl not sway Mr. Jones the borad was told.

Argonaut Insurance co. wants a 90-day Freeze but wont get it. (Quote) Argonaut may try

to claim a big debt or ttwo, we believe, Mr. jones said. Argonaut Personnel Director H.L.

Tupay said the Company will consider leaving the State by Apr. 1 if rebuffed.

. . . basics, continued

Make corrections in the following sentences by using the appropriate editing symbols.

1. The dicision by the two North African nation seemed to throw into question an major

agreementt reached Friday.

2. Fighting in a place public to the terror of the public is called an affray.

3. When a perosn accusde of a crime is taken before a courrt to plead to the chrge, he is

said to be arraigned.

4. When a person is held for questioning and but has not been charted, you run a risk

if you write that he has been arrested and for what reason.

5. The grand Jury will meet Wed. afternoon and thursday morn.

6. The President defended the invasion by Marines the invasion took place

only after all other options had been found unaceptable he said.

7. "I refuse to spend another moment on this assignment, the student said.

8. Every item of police news news should be verified before beingpublished.

9. 4 men ad one boy were needed to carry the sailboat mast.

10. The Best Time to plant flowers is in the Spring spring.

11. Marie mack, a girl of great talent played the piano when she was only three years old.

12. Grand juries hear ex parte evidence, and for just that reason all Grand jury proceedings

are to the public closed.

13. A person who recieves stolen property is usually called a FENCE.

14. what person says is more importat than how he say it.

Style

Style — Exercise 1

Didn't take you long to get through the part about symbols, did it? Actually, you aren't through. You will deal with editing symbols throughout the rest of this book. And then some. Now we add a little to the list of chores. You have to work on style.

Style provides a measure of consistency in any publication. It has no value of itself, being largely arbitrary. Still, adherence to some style guide gives readers a steady reference point. Someone may even think you know what you are doing.

This section is based on The Associated Press-United Press International stylebook. Correct all errors of style. DO NOT MAKE OTHER CHANGES.

1. Jones, who has a master's degree in Chemistry, wants a bachelors' degree in History.

2. Smith has a BA, MA, LL.D and Phd., I was told. (OK to abbreviate all.)

3. Dr. Farleigh Dickinson, Ph.d., is known as "Mr. Dickinson" by students and "Dick"

by intimates.

4. Elred lives at 5603 Lakemoore Dr, in Brightsville.

5. You get to Lakemoore Drive by turning left off Guadalupe St. and heading West.

6. If you live at 9 Lackawanna Ave., you have a prestigious address.

7. Lackawanna Avenue is parallel to East 42nd Street.

8. Few celebrities live there, except for David Bowie, who lives at 2,001 East 42nd St.

9. Bowie moved there from 1717 Fifth Avenue.

10. Before that, he lived on 6th ave.

11. The Colorado river makes a pronounced turn to the East as it flows past Brightsville.

Style — Exercise 2

A little style test. Correct all errors.

1. 243 freshpersons entered the college in 84, Dr. Martin Elred, professor of Journalism, said today at his office, which is a quarter-mile from his clasroom.

2. Dr. Elred, the 1st Nevadan on the Faculty, has ten goldfish, 6 cats, and 97 hamsters in his office. He is also a realtor; last month he sold four 4-room houses, ten three-room houses and twelve 10-room houses.

3. Elred walks four miles to school from his home on Denleavy Rd.; he even trudged through five inches of snow last Winter. He is 5 feet, 6 inches tall and has a 5 foot 11 inch wife. They have a rug 19 feet long (by 3 feet wide) in the home of their daughter, nineteen year old Betty, who lives at 1204 North Main Street but has a boyfriend, who works in Governor Bill Clements's Office and lives at 120 First St.

4. Friends live at 555 Lake Dr., 444 Creek avenue, 333 Ocean Boulevard, 222 Water lane, and 111 Water Terr.

5. If you get a bachelors degree at this school, it will be a BA in Journalism. That degree and a thumb will get you a ride on IH-35 or US 290 or RR 2222.

6. The Democratic party and the GOP gathered at fifth and Congress Streets.

7. In Marxism, theoreticians in Cardigan sweaters go to great lengths to show the decadence of French Fries and those quixotic Venetian blinds after 7PM.

8. He had a Danish, a little Polish sausage, some left-over pizza and an alkaseltzer.

9. In History classes, the profs often grade on a Curve.

Style — Exercise 3

Style: Capitalization, punctuation, addresses, titles. Correct all errors. Edit for style only.

1. Dr. S. Griffin Singer, a Journalism professor lives at 2713 Greenslope Avenue. He is a friend of Senator Allan Cranston (Dem., California), who will run for President.

2. At 4 East Riverside Dr. sits the Mansion of The Rev. Mr. Jesse Jones, pastor of Holiness Presbyterian church. On Williams St., just off Riverside, Professor Mike Quinn buy's Heineken Beer by the case, for the needy in The Turtle Creek Area of Dallas.

3. Prof. Mike Quinn, an Associate Dean in the Dean's Office of the college of communication at the Univ. of Texas was in the United Staes army at the time of the Korean Conflict. He served with Distinction and rose to the rank of Private First Class.

4. Pres. WilliamBurns has just moved into a new home at Eleven thirty-two Tumblebug Rd. which he and his wife, Belle, former Chairman of the Ad Department, must leave.

5. The Dept. of Journalism, headed by Chairman Maxwell McCombs, professor of Journalism, hits its peak in Sept. and Oct., heading for a December 12 completion, just before the Xmas Holidays and Final Exams.

6. In Green Bay, Wisconsin, and Detroit, Michigan, and Los Angeles, California, the bible is still on all Best--Seller Lists.

Style — Exercise 4

Get rid of the style errors in these sentences. Otherwise, do not edit them.

1. "I've said 100 times I'm not guilty, Johnson said

2. Damages were estimated at $750 thousand.

3. The six-year-old boy has been missing for ten days.

4. Firemen responded to a 3-alarm blaze in a warehouse at 1346 W. 8th St. at 6:00 p.m.

5. 62 fans were ejected from the stadium for rowdiness.

6. The page's actual dimensions were 6 3/16 inches x 13 11/32 inches.

7. He won the race in two hours, 36 minutes, 4 3/10 seconds.

8. They owned three cows, 12 horses, four pigs, and 22 goats.

9. The budget calls for an outlay of 7,998, 000 dollars.

10. He resigned after reading a 4000-word admission of guilt.

11. He hoped to avert World War 3 by adopting a hundred and six children. One

hundred, thirty-three applied.

12. 1986 was a good year, particularly in the Summer.

13. The priest argued that the Christian Religion was doomed, but the Rabbi disagreed.

14. He said he felt like Jesus, who was betrayed by one of His followers.

15. The basic style rule calls for spelling out numbers below ten and using figures for

those of 10 and above.

Style — Exercise 5

More style. This one concentrates on capitalization. It has some other errors, too, so you should stay on your toes and change them all. Do not rephrase the sentences.

1. He went to Texas A &M after leaving Southern Illinois.

2. She bought her books at waldenbooks.

3. Gov. Preston Smith was the guest of Attorney General Crawford Martin and the university Chancellor, Hans Mark.

4. Prof. Joe Winters, who teaches Journalism, has written a new novel, "What are we waiting for"? He also writes radio scripts for Travis county.

5. D. Claud Bowers flew to Long Beach, California Tuesday. He arrived at 6 am. and took a Taxi to Jones's house.

6. Mary's first date was with Joe Gruene, Jr., who once lived at the Y.M.C.A. while working for Time Magazine and Radio Station K-NOW.

7. In the early 1970's, he made a few A's at the University, but then he ran into trouble with Charles Dicken's stories when he pledged the Sigma Nu's.

8. He learned that Merle Oberon, a Black Power advocate from the panhandle, got 25% of his salary--a hundred dollars a day--from the Rotary club.

9. The sophomore girl worked for Mr. Joe Raggan, selling an alcoholic drink mixed of rum & coke.

10. The Post Office delivers 1,000s of letters daily to First National Bank of Longview.

11. Four Nations, all members of the United Nations, back the africans.

12. A celluloid collar can trouble you as you drink dr pepper or tequilla.

13. I used to drive a Buick LeSabre, but I switched to a Sedan.

14. Students from the Midwest move south for cheaper tuition at College.

15. Winds from the north often threaten Longviewers with frostbite.

16. Storms usually move from west to East because of the way the Earth turns on its Axis,

a nobel Prize Winner told a group of US Marines.

17. In the Pacific and Indian Oceans, you can get a Sunburn that hurts like Hell.

18. These studetns excell in History, Journalism and English Literature after the Civil war.

Or was that the Korean War? Or World War One?

19. As a Government major, you get a lot of Asian History, especially intwo classes,

Asian History 370 and 376.

20. Read the bible, talmud and Koran for enlightenment. Your AP stylebook is your

journalism bible. It has notes on Biblical references.

21. All Black students who support Christianity can go to the student union for a visit with

Coach Fred Ochstrow at 4 PM Thurs.

Style — Exercise 6

Now we move to some regular stories for our work with style. Correct all style errors in these stories by using proper symbols. The stories will appear in your student newspaper.

A journalism senior from Chicago, Illinois, will join Governor Will Waite's headquarters staff February 4th. The student, Lisa, Lhasa, will direct purchasing for the March 2 and Apr. 21st celebrations.

The gov. said Miss Lhasa, who lives at 1702 West Eleventh Street, will also coordinate celebrations with former residents of the state who now live in Oklahoma, Minn., and Arkansas. A maid from Athens, Texas and one from Los Angeles, Calif., will help Lhasa. One of those aids lives on Maple Rd. and the other lives at 1,222 Penn Drive, having moved there not long ago from Boston. Massachusetts.

* * *

Dr. Martin Elred, Professor of Journalism, has asket Lieut. Gov. Bill hobby to speak to his Journalism class February 14. ; Elred will be out of town then, attending the Annual Convention of the National Newspaper Association. Elred is on the Association Board. He gets twenty cents a mile for travel to board meetings.

For $10,000,000, Dr. Elred would give up that job, he said. He has had an offer from the Federal Communications Commission to be an F.C.C. trouble-shooter in Saint Louis.

Style — Exercise 7

Mark style corrections in the following stories by using the correct editing symbols.   Correct all errors, but do not reword the sentences. Be sure to mark all paragraphs.

Regular exercise that burns up two thousand calories a week appears to reduce the risk of premature death by heart attack.

Researchers have found that men who exercised off 2,000 calories a week had a 28% lower death rate than less active men. The sixteen-year study was conducted with a group of college men. The 16396 participants ranged in age from 35 to 74.

The research indicates that even people with high blood pressure benefit from exercise. For instance, men with high blood pressure who burned off 2000 calories a week had less than 1/2 the risk of death as those who exercised the least.

* * *

Brightsville schools will conduct an attendance contest this year to try to boost state aid. Students will be able to win t shirts while the School District gets more State money.

School Supt. Burl Osburne said attendance dropped five percentage points last year to 94.5 per cent. Much state aid is based on attendance.

Supt. Osburne said the district is looking at both a major tax increase and major budget cuts for the next fiscal year. "We are looking at everything," he said. "There are no sacred cows."

President of the Brightsville Association of Teachers Donna Knowe said there may be no pay raises next year.

* * *

The Mexican government Thurs. nearly doubled the price of tortillas, the mainstay of the mexican diet, in an effort to trim subsidies in the budget.

Consumers, already struggling with double-digit inflation, immediately complained about the increase, which boosted the price from sixty-five pesos a kilogram to 95. That works out to a jump from about eight cents to fifteen cents for about 22.2 pounds—43 tortillas.

Poor families may qualify for special coupons provided through unions and the government-owned food company, Conasupo. Coupons entitle them to tortillas for fifty pesos, or about six cents a kilogram. The government has agreed to raise the minimum wage 25.1 per cent, starting the first of next month, in an effort to help workers keep pace with higher costs.

* * *

If Brightsville approves and private donations of at least 10,000 dollars can be raised, the city's green water towar at 600 West 1st Street may soon look mighty like a rose.

. . . **exercise 7,** continued

"It'll be a tribute to Art Greenspan who is responsible for a lot of Brightsville's image," Brightsville Arts Commission Chairman Harold Clapper told members of the commission Wed.

The Commission voted to pass the idea along to a subcommittee that makes recommendations on art in public places. If the subcommittee supports the idea and the Commission concurs, the city council will be urged to okay it.

* * *

The President said yesterday that the only people who go hungry in America are those who do not know where or how to get help.

"I don't think there is anyone going hungry in America simply by reason of denial or lack of ability to feed them," the President told a group of High School students in Washington, DC. A student asked the President about the cuts in federal funds for education. The President saidstudent loan guarantees are at an alltime high, but he admitted scholarships are tougher to get.

". . . Its true there are scholarship's, and there well should be. But there's something else: There's nothing wrong with working at jobs at the same time you're going to school. I say this because I worked my way through College," the president said

* * *

Style — Exercise 8

Edit these stories as your instructor suggests.

Officials were optimistic Mon. that navy ports will be established on the Gulf Coastdespite a Senate panel's vote against the idea of home ports across the country.

In two 9-9 votes, the Senate armed services committee defeated a motion to authorize construction funds for home ports in Washington State and New York, going against the concept of home ports.

Funds already have been approved to renovate the battleship U.S.S. Wisconsisn, that would anchor a fleet of vessels including an aircraft carrier, a guided missile cruiser and aguided missile destroyer in Corpus Christ, Tex.

Sen. Phil Gramm (Rep. Tex.) said support for Gulf home ports was strong because of stratetic concerns inthe face of a growing presence of the USSR in the Gulf of Mexico.

Gramm, a member of the Armed services committee, said that sixty per cent of all supplies going from the U.S. to Europe in the event of war would come from gulf ports. He said there is a growing threat of russian maneuvers in Cuba that could require United States Naval power in the gulf and that the home ports would "help project Naval power" into Central America where Nicaragua is a potential Russian base.

* * *

Teamsters President Jackie Tomas won overwhelming election Fri. to his first 5-year term as head of the Union.

Tomas was indicted last week on charges of racketeering and embezzlement. Tomas, 59 has been head of the Teamsters--the nation's largest union--since 1983 through an interimappointment by a seventeen-member Executive Board oafter his predecessor, Roy Williams, was convicted of trying to bribe a United States Senator.

A 1984 law passed by Congress following the conviction of Williams prohibits anyone convicted of a felony from holding union office.

* * *

Two art appraisers say Salvador Dali's own greed lies bhehind much of the confusion about the authenticity of his limited edition prints. The onus is on Mr. Dali, who for the past fifty years "has been recognized as an extremely avaricious individual," said Jackson Ninuk, an appraiser in Brightsville. "Dali is the one who has allowed these practices to go on." It's for him and his crowd of groupiesto put out a catalogue and solve the problem-- just as you have a catalog for Picasso and Miro and Chagall and Rembrandt."

The discussion was spurred by the removal of eleven Dali prints, said to be fake, from Shelby Fine Arts Gallery inColorado Springs, Colorado, Apr. 9. Police said the works were printed on paper with a watermark that was not in use until 1982, although the spanish-born Dali stopped signing lithographs in '79. Nunik and Brightsville Appraiser Ewell Renard said, however, that the controversy about Dali prints has been going on for

... **exercise 8**, continued

years. In 1978, German customs officials seized 40,000 blank sheets of paper signed by Dali, Nuniksaid.

"Dali learned he could sell his signature for $40 per blank sheet in the mid-1970's, "Nunik said. " By signing his name every 2 seconds he produced 1,800 sheets an hour. There wer probably 350,000 blank sheeets of paper signed by Dali," Nunik said. Renard said pricing Dali prints is as complex as determining authenticity. A print called The Disappearing Bust of Aristotle is priced from $300 to $2200, depending on the dealer, and Exploding Madonna goes for $399 to $6500.

* * *

An 18-month old Brightsville boy who drowned in a swimming pool at the family home was identified today as Michael Cuellar.

The child was found Wednesday night in the pool at 2,400 North Broad Boulevard.

The child had been out of sight of relatives for about fifteen minutes when they found him in the pool, said police sergeant John Cochran." Relatives said that when he was found, the boy had no heartbeat nor respiration.

* * *

A six-month-old Brightsville girl is recovering after a liver transplant, a MemorialHospital spokesperson said Wednesday.

... **exercise 8,** continued

The patient, Kay Flawn, was in critical condition after the operation ended at 4:00 p.m., said spokesperson Mary Jane Bodie. "Everything went well," Bodie said. "we expect a full recovery."

Flawn was the sixth person to receive a liver transplant at the hospital.

* * *

Fire Department investigators have found 2 bodies in the rubble of a Mobile Home that burned down Sunday Morning. A 3rd body is being sought.

The victims were Mrs. Cherry Charise, 24, and her a 6 year old daughter, Winsome. And 18-month-old son, Chester, is missing and is presumed to have died in the fire.

The blaze was reported at 2:17 AM Sunday morning. Firefighters were concerned about bullets flying around from rifle ammunition that exploded when heated. No fireighter was injured.

Another resident of the home, David McKnack, 38, was sleeping when the fire started. He suffered second- and third-degree burns on both arms and hands.

The home was parked permanently in the Elred Trailer Manse, 1801 Manor Downs Road.

Grammar

Your name _____

Date _____

Grammar — word problems

The following sentences contain examples of some of the most common word problems in news writing. Use the appropriate editing symbols to make corrections. Do not rephrase.

1. The person who's name is called last may go to the head of the line.

2. The price of the tires was upped 40 percent overnight.

3. The sidewalk which is in need of repair is in front of the house at 2400 Broad Ave.

4. The memento from Thailand is among the most unique of souvenirs in her collection.

5. The Democrats that were dissatisfied bolted the convention.

6. The spectator was reticent to appear as a witness for either party in the auto accident.

7. The senator took the floor to refute the charges of his colleague.

8. The board voted to postpone further spending until the interest on the principle fell to 6 percent.

9. The City Council enacted an ordinance against peddling in residential areas.

10. The affect of the tax measure will not be felt until the end of next year.

11. The fugitive alluded capture longer than he had hoped.

12. Brightsville businessmen will sponsor the first annual job festival this summer.

13. Major legislation in Congress was thwarted this session by a coalition of the rural and resort blocks.

14. Seniors, who comprise the biggest group, are expected to lead the team.

15. The altercation in the bar left one man with a bloody nose and one with a concussion.

16. The contractor refused to honor the verbal agreement between him and the homeowner.

17. An artillery barrage completely destroyed the farmhouse.

18. Apples are different than oranges, although the two often are confused during arguments.

19. The old man remained in good health due to exercise, but he liked to give the credit to his diet.

20. The district attorney inferred to the jury that the physician was a quack, but the jury missed the point.

21. Prior to this year, only persons with incomes below $20,000 were eligible.

22. Less than 100 people turned out for the free concert.

23. A person who flaunts the rules of society is likely to be known as a "scofflaw."

24. The lumber which was stacked over 50 feet high was in danger of tumbling down.

25. An edge in the night air promised cooler temperatures by morning.

26. The proposal for a tax increase brought heavy flack from Brightsville voters.

27. After the preacher prepared his sermon, he laid down for a nap.

28. Records indicate that five U.S. flyers remain prisoners of the Vietnamese.

29. G.T. Martin will retire as a U.S. marshall after 30 years.

30. The dead trees looked like sentinels, and the ground looked like it had been brushed with poison.

Grammar — sound-alikes

Homophones are words that have the same sound but differ in spelling, origin and meaning. The following sentences contain homophones frequently encountered in news writing. Choose the correct ones.

1. The Hun leader sent his hoards/hordes against the helpless villagers.

2. The principle/principal cause of poor grades is lack of motivation.

3. The main source of cholesterol in eggs is in the yoke/yolk.

4. The seal is to be evaluated in the spring for release onto an ice flow/floe.

5. The Zirkel band features saxophones, trombones, trumpets, clarinets, drums, base/bass and piano.

6. Before turning to a life of crime, Elred was an alter/altar boy.

7. Metal objects placed into a microwave oven may cause an electrical ark/arc.

8. The candy sticks are 4 cents a piece/apiece.

9. Let us put this job aside for awhile/a while.

10. The auger/augur was taken from his box of tools in the garage.

11. The captain is expected to order anchors away/aweigh at any moment.

12. She promised sarcastically to wait with baited/bated breath.

13. The winter freeze left the fertile land baron/barren.

14. The romance between the two thespians was called bizarre/bazaar because of the differences in their ages.

15. Something about a day at the beech/beach gives it universal appeal.

16. We should avoid cliches, such as references to the "bear facts/bare facts."

17. The reviewer described the play as the most boaring/boring of the season.

18. He quit the bank to take a job as a hot dog vender/vendor.

19. Efforts to rescue the child were all in vane/vain.

20. The only solution is to tow/toe the car.

21. The officer hoped to be reassigned to the vice/vise squad.

22. The convict lost his trustee/trusty status after an altercation with a guard.

23. The developer bought three tracks/tracts of land just south of the

Vermillion River.

24. The bombers flew threw/through a sky thick with flak/flack.

25. The derogatory term for a press agent is a flak/flack.

26. Two witnesses said the gunman had a slight tic/tick below the right eye.

27. The injured whale was clearly in the throws/throes of death.

28. The shallow pool was teeming/teaming with tadpoles.

29. The woman was a little too straight-laced/strait-laced to suit the gambler.

30. The banker felt good about the deal, and he demanded his just deserts/desserts.

31. The driver failed to set the break/brake and the car rolled into the lake.

32. The company has been looking more than a month for a cite/site for a new office.

33. The generator has to be installed on a stationary/stationery platform before it may be

operated safely.

. . . **sound-alikes,** continued

34. Mark Oct. 25 on your calendar/calender.

35. Officials will complete the election canvas/canvass in two weeks.

36. The state capitol/capital is constructed of marble and granite.

37. The coach clinched/clenched his teeth and kept his temper.

38. The divorce suit named the journalism professor as the correspondent/corespondent.

39. The soldier was not fazed/phased by the close call.

40. Insects are dyeing/dying by the thousands as a result of the spraying.

41. The job called for someone who knew how to be discreet/discrete and subtle.

42. The program was established to have a duel/dual benefit for the participants and the community.

43. President Reagan showed a flare/flair for the dramatic.

44. The president's wife said she felt faint/feint and asked to be excused.

45. The gated/gaited horse was not as well groomed as the racehorse.

46. The life of a sheep is not a constant gambol/gamble, as poets sometimes lead us to believe.

47. The cowboy led/lead the horses to water, but he could not make them drink.

48. The suspects were indited/indicted on three charges of fraud.

49. Others are loath/loathe to give up something that yields so much political good will.

50. The day of the hippie/hippy and the flower child is gone forever.

Grammar — diction

In the following sentences, the word or phrase in bold type does not convey the precise idea or thought it should. Supply the correct word or phrase by using the appropriate editing symbols . Be especially vigorous in deleting pomposities and general grandiosity. Make other changes only if required by the change in a boldface word.

1. Two peace activists convicted of damaging military computer equipment at a Brightsville plant were **sentenced to** probation Thursday by a federal judge.

2. A Brightsville pimp convicted last week of murdering a **competitor** was sentenced Thursday to 11 years in prison.

3. Orlando Kalcan, a Brightsville Democrat, **repeated his willingness** to increase the state sales tax and support legalized gambling.

4. Few reporters have handy sources they can call on Sunday afternoon to **inquire** about the psychological roots of procrastination.

5. Both would require the city to **purchase** right of way on homes and businesses.

6. As the doctor injected the victim with two bottles of **anti-venom**, he spoke frankly about chances for recovery.

7. The revolver, the drugs, the gems, and about 12,000 other items came from unclaimed **safety deposit** boxes.

8. The fight has gone to Congress where **laws** to ban the gray market have been introduced in both the House and Senate.

9. The arguments offered to support both pro and **anti** positions are plentiful, but the facts can be obscured by hyperbole.

... **diction**, continued

10. Brightsville's choices of land parcels up for annexation are expected to be **prioritized** later this month.

11. He says, "Look, I'm an illegal alien," and they have him picked up. They are cutting off their nose **despite** their face.

12. Slade and his sons were aboard a Jordanian airliner when it was **commandeered** Tuesday in Beirut by Lebanese gunmen.

13. Shirley Downs, the retired director of the Brightsville Library, was honored by Central College, of which she is an **alumnus.**

14. Grant, who served as a Central County deputy from January 1975 until December 1976, also **received a probated sentence** of five years for forging a $757 refund check from the Internal Revenue Service.

15. John Davetson **succumbed to** cancer at the age of 14.

16. Rep. Sweeney Coldfarb of Brightsville told his colleagues that his grandmother is such a **died-in-the-wool** Democrat that she was barely able to vote for him.

17. **The** *El Sol de Mexico* newspaper said Maria Luisa Segura was Bravo Cervantes' wife and the two men were her sons.

18. A decision to delay the project was made **following** talks with two utility companies.

19. A Central State School therapist died when her car **collided** with a brick wall about 7:15 a.m. east of Central City.

. . . diction, continued

20. The accident **took place** at 2:15 a.m. June 30.

21. The wedding will **occur** Feb. 29 in accordance with the bride's wishes.

22. The investigation **into** a vandalized painting at the Brightsville Museum of Art is now complete but has yielded no results.

23. The attack **occurred** a day after an Iranian jet fighter fired a rocket at a Kuwaiti boat.

24. Although the cause of the stroke has not been determined, there was a 95 percent chance it was caused by a clot that formed around the artificial heart and **migrated** to a blood vessel in the head, Dr. Devries said.

25. Now the candidate wonders if he can become the first presidential aspirant since Richard Nixon in 1968 to ride into the White House on accusations of misconduct of foreign affairs as **a cutting issue.**

26. A second mission is to **insert and extract** individuals or small commando units involved in quick-strike, clandestine attacks behind enemy lines.

27. In a steady decline since early this year, the pound has lost 66 percent of its value **vis-a-vis** the U.S. dollar.

28. Brightsville police were attempting late Wednesday to **locate** Johnson—who has been living under a different name—and serve her the warrant.

29. With a screenplay by Pat Proft and himself, director Neal Israel's film **centers around** the dozen or so students who have sped, collided or otherwise **violated themselves** into a compulsory driving course.

... **diction**, continued

30. The newspaper said Lucas would have had to travel thousands of miles in short time periods to **carry out** the more than 210 slayings with which he has been **credited.**

31. Officials were quoted as saying that two of the 15 **murders** attributed to Lucas in California probably were committed by others.

32. When the Chinese reached the South Korean fishing boat, six of the 19 crewmen were dead **from** gunshot wounds.

33. One member of the group told the committee that her son had been killed in a wreck caused by a **drunk** driver.

34. Peak demand is a key indicator because utility companies must have adequate generating capacity available or be able to buy power in times of highest **usage.**

35. But **traditionally** rainy April was one of the driest in 100 years.

36. Hernandez said he has resigned from the Brown Berets because its bylaws **prohibit** members to seek political office.

37. The president will make a visit to China next year, the secretary of state **divulged** Wednesday.

38. Debbi Smith, who was stabbed and beaten in her apartment last month, was **released** from the hospital Friday.

39. When the project will be **instigated** will depend on funding and the whim of the council.

40. The "Pablo scale" went into use in 1983 to measure an inmate's chances of success **in the free world.**

41. The fire was then directed **further** south, where the Israeli army controls a village.

42. The 114 shipments from western New York will be among the first since a **de facto** moratorium on the transportation of nuclear waste began in the 1970s.

43. The fair has 32 outstanding dealers of **quality** antiques.

44. Cuban President Fidel Castro said the deadline was delayed two days to help the public make **alternate** travel arrangements.

45. The attorney general **persuaded** the jury that the defendant, who was 16 at the time, was overcome by uncontrollable rage.

46. Diplomats said that the vote on the invasion of Grenada was equal in **impact** to the 1980 anti-Soviet vote.

47. The fighting left 50 Cubans **injured** and an undetermined number dead.

48. The suit seeks injunctions **forbidding** the city **from** refusing parade permits.

49. Revenue bonds are **repaid** from rates charged by the utility, airport or hospital.

50. AIDS usually afflicts male homosexuals, who **comprise** about 75 percent of the victims, but drug users, blood tranfusion recipients and Haitian immigrants also get it.

51. Bail totaling $200,000 was set Thursday **on** a Brightsville resident being held in the shooting that ended with the death of a state trooper.

... **diction,** continued

52. Both agencies will announce their ratings **prior to** the sale.

53. Moments after the debate, commissioners voted 3-1 to **hike** their pay to $52,000.

54. The names of the dead were **released** by the sheriff two days after the accident.

55. Residents who fail to pay back taxes will be sued and may lose their property, the tax

collector **warned**.

56. A favorable report by a federal licensing panel **should** improve the city's chances to

get out of the project.

57. The exchange is overburdened, a problem that makes it **tough** to place and receive

calls during certain hours.

58. The Brightsville Lutheran Church **sustained** $500,000 in damage Tuesday in a three-

alarm fire.

59. The FBI is sponsoring a crime detection seminar, which will be open **for free** to the

public.

60. The suicide rate among young Americans climbed during the 1980s, and federal health

researchers **have launched** a study to try to find out why.

61. The driver suffered **abrasions and contusions** in the accident.

62. The burglary was reported to police **around** noon.

63. After a search of three weeks deputies found the **decomposed** body in a cotton field.

64. Neither **doctors** nor dentists support the new Medicare proposals.

... **diction,** continued

65. The airplane **mishap** is considered the worst in aviation history.

66. The grand jury foreman refused to say what had **transpired** during the session.

67. The **suspect** rose as the judge prepared to pronounce the sentence.

68. The home was **gutted** by fire.

69. The game was over **at approximately** 7 p.m.

70. He emphasized that all available personnel are involved in the **probe** of the slaying.

71. "Jimmy Dean" is a triumph—a **masterful** blend of humor and heartbreak.

72. Neither city charter nor state law contained a **method** to assure that the utility firms would be fairly compensated.

73. County employes have accumulated $107,000 in overtime pay, but that money was not to be **dispersed** until the commissioners ordered it.

74. The woman whose house was **burgled** said an attorney general's investigator questioned them last week about the break-in.

75. The program is expected to be **finalized** tomorrow and sent to the board.

76. The reason the job costs so much is **because** the part is priced so high.

77. In one incident an inmate was refused **medication** because the doctor could not compile the necessary **documentation**.

78. Two police officers were wounded while trying to **apprehend** Lowry and his companion in connection with the robbery in a Brightsville suburb.

...**diction,** continued

79. Police **were seeking a suspect** who shot two clerks at a drive-in grocery.

80. The ambulances **rushed** the victims to a nearby hospital.

81. The new copy editor **with** the newspaper **is a recent** journalism graduate.

82. The driver **sustained** injuries severe enough to **required** hospitalization.

83. The professor was glad to take a new **position** at another school.

84. When alcohol nurtures anger, trouble is almost **inevitable.**

85. The convicts **staged** a three-hour riot.

86. Three of the victims of the train wreck remain **unnamed.**

87. The defendant **claimed** to be innocent, but the jury did not believe him.

88. The GOP **anticipates** Democratic support on the tax bill.

89. His foot, **compared to** mine, is small.

90. **Poundwise,** the purchase was considered a bargain.

91. All the **burglars** who robbed the bank were armed with automatic weapons.

92. The **final** decision will be left to the president.

93. Mothers Against Drunk Driving has had an effect on **drunk** driving, but the name of

the group does not do much to help correct language usage.

94. The deal with the state's attorney was completed Monday when the mother pleaded

guilty of injury to a child.

95. A man at the animal shelter said the doe was **euthanized** because it was suffering.

... diction, continued

96. The announcement was made in Brightsville on a **local r**adio station.

97. A rescue squad found the bodies Monday of three children who **were drowned** Sunday after they waded into deep water.

98. Despite the **enormity** of the increase sought by the telephone company, only 18 persons appeared to protest the proposal.

99. A few seconds made Jack Dempsey a winner, a loser and a **myth**.

100. The jury **handed down** a verdict after three hours of deliberation.

Grammar — elegance

The practice of using a word phrase to avoid repeating a substantive is known as *elegant variation,* and it afflicts news writers of all levels. Some reporters having written *elephant* will almost always write *pachyderm* on second reference. Such preoccupation often leads to ridiculous phrasing and outrageous composition. The solution is to repeat the original word or to use a pronoun. In this passage from a newspaper, elegant variation is taken to the extreme:

> A bank teller was being held on $100,000 bail Monday in the embezzlement of $45,000 from the Brightsville National Bank.
> A bank examiner said he obtained a confession from the one-time football star.
> Bank officials said they found it difficult to believe that the serious-minded Sunday school teacher had taken the money.
> The GI trainee told investigators he took the job to earn money to go into business for himself.
> The former YMCA boy's counselor admitted he had lost money in stock speculation.
> The son of a former clergyman denied that women played a part in the theft.
> The former paratrooper said he would ask none of his friends to go his bail.

In your work as a copy editor, you will have to keep other people out of that elegant trap. Let's try that with the following sentences.

1. The snow accumulation is at 6 feet, and more of the white fluffy stuff is forecast.

2. The price of bananas has reached 75 cents a pound, and grocers said in another month shoppers who buy the elongated yellow fruit will have to pay at least $1 a pound.

3. Snuffy the cat is one feline that has made good use of nine lives.

4. An elephant never forgets, but what does a pachyderm have to remember?

5. For an unexplained reason, 200 whales beached themselves, and authorities say the mammals will all die.

6. Despite its ignorance the opossum has survived for years, but now the only North

American marsupial is being threatened by the spread of cities.

To continue, we look at some briefer examples of elegance--just a word or two—and some useless words. Replace the fancy terms with normal terms. Some of the sentences can be improved simply by eliminating the offending word.

7. He **purchased** four guns and 10 boxes of shells.

8. All available ambulances were **immediately dispatched** to the scene of the tragedy.

9. The building was rocked by a **violent** explosion.

10. The thieves **gained entrance** through a skylight.

11. He said he had not **yet** received the report.

12. Construction work has **already** begun.

13. The witness denied **any** knowledge of the robbery.

14. The senator is **now** serving his third term.

15. The house burned **down.**

16. The flight set a **new** altitude record.

17. She strangled **to death.**

18. He **serves as** vice president.

19. The teacher had a **bad** cold.

20. The ambulance **transported** Grindstone to Memorial Hospital.

21. Kelley was coated with **a mixture of** petroleum jelly, lamp black and shark repellent

before diving into the water from the island.

Grammar — a little quiz

Make corrections in diction and grammar in the following sentences as appropriate.

1. Cooler temperatures and rain from Hurricane Danny are expected to reduce water consumption substantially.

2. An Oregon resident is the only survivor of a one-car collision near this Central Missouri town.

3. The Brightsville residents quickly launched a boat, and Baker dove in where he had see the swimmer go under.

4. The company's headquarters are in Brightsville.

5. One reason that Chapman may find a Commerce Committee assignment hard to get is because three Arkansas Democrats already serve on the committee.

6. With clinical skill, Digs lays bear the machinations of the nuclear family as loveless marriages, sibling rivalries and pathetic senility provide the battleground.

7. Every effort must be made to increase adequately professional skills and attainments.

8. In the last 10 years, there have been an average of 22 accidents annually.

9. Eleven of the 18 candidates will be arrested if they do not pay a fine of 7 billion pesos each for getting less than 50,000 votes.

10. One of the students fell on a stairway in the capital while in the Senate chamber.

11. She got the idea from a visit to Ireland, where a politician explained how a psychic located a runaway monkey by feeling vibrations from a map.

12. So far, an estimated 3.5 million acres of a total of 5 million acres have been sprayed,

an effort which officials have estimated will cost $3 an acre.

13. Neither Walker nor Whitworth have cooperated with prosecutors, and their lack of

cooperation has frustrated efforts to make a full assessment of the damage.

14. During Ronald Reagan's first term, he and his aides gave a masterful display of the art

of manipulating the press.

15. Two marshals aboard the aircraft subdued the gunman and prevented the plane from

being commandeered.

16. Moments after the holdup, the gunmen were apprehended.

17. The commissioner urged taxpayers to contact legislators about adding a cent to the

sales tax and designate it for county coffers.

18. The house payment of $745 includes only principle and interest.

19. A rash of bombings has led to an order that all officers wear flack jackets on patrol.

20. The mayor studied the city manager's report and mistakenly implied that a tax increase

would be necessary.

21. When drugs are mixed with alcohol, the affects can be deadly.

22. Gramm suggested banning company cars and the elimination of other fringe benefits.

23. It is like the song says: "The farther you go, the more sorrow you know."

24. The wreck took place about 12:45 p.m. Monday four miles south of Brightsville.

25. A doctor of great skill, the patient considered himself in good hands.

26. Only an uninterested arbitrator is likely to make an impartial judgment.

27. None of the children on the bus was seriously injured in the crash.

28. Despite all their efforts, not one of the top five or six players were able to make the shot three times in a row.

29. On cross-examination, the defense attorney inferred that Jones knew his partner was forging the checks.

30. The defeated fighter is all ready in training for the rematch.

31. The commission ruling will effect the new tax rate much more than first expected.

32. The next Super Bowl is expected to attract over 150,000 fans.

33. President Reagan said him and Nancy preferred to go to Camp David.

34. Almost everyone from the White House was going except Reagan and she.

35. The reason the student missed class was because she overslept.

36. The terrorist threats failed to frighten Ellen and I.

37. The reward could not be divided between the three detectives to their full satisfaction.

38. The baby laid quietly for a long time and listened to the voices in the other room.

39. The district attorney wondered who's coat had been left in place of his own.

40. The woefully neglected building seems to be sighing in sadness from it's roof to its sagging porch.

41. The Cabinet member said if he was president he would take a different approach.

42. Neither the president or a majority of his aides favored an air attack.

43. Each of the Cabinet members was permitted to express their opinion.

44. The convict could not convince his attorney to file an appeal.

45. The children at camp tiptoed passed the sleeping counselor.

46. It is generally accepted that a mixture of different varieties of apples—probably four or five—make the best cider.

47. Housewise, a buyer is better off with three bedrooms than with two.

48. Snow fell for the third day, but the children could not seem to get enough of the fluffy white stuff.

49. The father urged his son to become a doctor or a dentist.

50. The captain judged the distance to be 1,000 yards, but to the soldiers it seemed much further.

Syntax

Your name _____

Date _____

Syntax — pronouns

Demands of speed and brevity in news writing lead to fractured syntax uncommon in most other forms of writing. Still, it is not enough to write so that the reader will know what we mean. We should try to write *precisely* what we mean.

Misplaced relative pronouns frequently cause problems. You need some practice in getting your pronouns lined up. Here it comes: Edit the following sentences to improve the syntax by placing the relative pronoun next to the word it modifies. Be careful not to change the sense of the sentence. Make two sentences only in desperation. (We will focus on the problems of wordiness later, and you will get to make two or even three sentences out of some long-winded sentences.)

1. Grand Duke Jean Valjean of Luxembourg has paid tribute to the 4th Infantry Division of Fort Carson, Colo., which liberated his homeland during World War II, noting that the division lost one third of its men in a year.

2. In the aftermath, the imperious Connally was not the welcome White House guest in the first four years of the self-contained Reagan administration that he had been during the Nixon and Ford administrations.

3. Last year the cycle was disrupted by hard freezes in January and February that damaged lawn grasses and shrubbery.

4. Bricks from the old building at 15th Street and Interregional Highway, which was demolished last fall, will be on sale for $7.

5. Three undercover officers for the city, who wore bulletproof vests and windbreakers, got the three men out of their car, handcuffed them and drove them off.

6. Members of an animal protection agency are upset about a live pigeon shoot in Central City last weekend that left 50 dead or dying birds on the roof of a home.

. . . pronouns, continued

7. Federal health researchers said Thursday that women of child-bearing age in the United States who cannot have children fit a distinct statistical pattern.

8. Although the candidates have filed, the city is awaiting a federal court ruling on the legality of the at-large election system, which could delay the elections April 7.

9. Sgt. Dave Kesyl of the Brightsville Police Department estimated that 250 traffic accidents were reported Friday and Saturday in the city, which he said is above average.

10. The Senate agreed Tuesday to keep a $2 million tax break for two mysterious investors that was placed in the tax reform bill by GOP Sen. William Armstrong of Colorado.

11. Meanwhile, an effort by Sen. Paul Trible of Vermont to retain a special pension tax break for 20 million workers, most of them in government, who contribute to their own retirement, was rejected.

12. The Republican professional assessed Baker's chances by quoting the baseball man in the novel *Bang the Drum Slowly* who says of weak pitchers that they could win a few games "if God drops everything else."

13. Earlier Friday, the Senate refused to change a provision in the bill that would prohibit taxpayers who do not file itemized returns from deducting charitable contributions.

14. The two players from the Brightsville Community College basketball team who have been accused of shaving points have left school.

15. In response to criticism by many voters that the old system involved too much red tape, the legistlator introduced a bill to make the process easier.

Your name _____

Date _____

Syntax — *only*

The word *only* is perhaps the peskiest in the language. It editorializes and distorts with uncanny subtlety. For example, you can produce seven meanings just by placing the word in different positions in the following sentence. Try it with this sentence from *The Elements of Style* by Strunk and White:

I hit him in the eye yesterday.

Such a sentence might reach a copy editor in any one of the seven versions. Edit the following sentences by deleting *only* or moving it to a more appropriate position in the sentence.

1. Children under 16 get in free and those over 16 only pay a dollar.

2. The mayor said he only wanted what is best for the city.

3. The housing project will cost $1.5 million, but the board only appropriated $1 million.

4. Mexico only defaulted on its loan payment to the World Bank; other producing nations paid promptly.

5. The defendant, who is 17 years old, received only five years in prison for his part in the slaying.

6. The boy only had to walk two blocks to school and his parents opposed the transfer.

7. Take the train only if that is the quickest way to reach San Francisco from Brightsville.

8. Records only showed two homeowners in arrears on payments to the association.

9. The witness testified that she could only remember the details before the accident happened.

10. The driver insisted that he was sober because he only drank two light beers while he was at the party.

Your name _____

Syntax — *not only*

Date _____

Now let's look at *not only.* The trick: The words affected by *not only* have to be the same kind of words--two nouns, two verbs, two whatevers. For example:

He is not only tall but handsome. Two adjectives.
He not only sings but dances. Two verbs.
It went not only to Smith but to Wesson. Two objects, nouns.

Try one yourself. Put the *not only* where it does the job right:

1. The commission not only demanded that education be free but also that free

transportation and housing be provided.

(You must put the *not only* behind *demanded.* Or you must get another verb: He not only demanded that education be free but insisted. . . . Let's try some more.)

2. It has not only a life of its own but has years of tradition behind it.

3. Surgery involves not only the removal of all of the foot but also much of the leg.

4. They talk as if the United States were not only encouraging the militarism of Israel but

also the development of a Israeli atomic bomb.

5. The country's second largest retailing chain has not only decided to remain but also to

expand its staff in Brightsville.

6. He not only fought Archie Moore twice but also Rocky Marciano.

7. NTSU has signed not only four tackles but also had oral commitments from two backs.

8. These questions not only give me a headache but also a large pain in the back.

9. The map showed not only Malaysia's vulnerability but also depicted clearly its strategic

role in the ASEAN defense approach.

10. The coffee was not only bitter but it had grown cold.

Syntax — *that*

In news writing, the word *that* after certain verbs of attribution, especially *said*, has become known as a culprit to be consigned to oblivion. A lot of the time it should be, but sometimes it is needed to avoid ambiguity, especially when the *said* verb is transitive. Take this sentence for example: "The professor warned the semiliterates would throw the world into an ambiguous chaos if left to their own devices." A *that* is clearly needed after *warned.* The professor is not warning the semiliterates. He is warning *that* the semiliterates may adversely influence the language. In the following sentences, supply *that* when it is needed and delete *that* when not needed. Some sentences need no change.

1. Elizabeth Chagra testified that the gunman was neither her husband nor her brother.

2. The president said that the invasion of Grenada would tell the world that the United States stands for freedom and justice.

3. The officer told the protesters that they would have to move on.

4. The sailors were warned that the storm would reach their position in less than an hour.

5. The suspect denied that Betty Smith did it.

6. The detective added cyanide was also thought to be one of the poisons.

7. The convicts shouted the warden was a nerd.

8. The officer said that the driver and all the passengers would have to go to city hall.

9. The trainer said he knew that the dog's long ears and odd-shaped tail—two points that the judges always consider—would probably hurt its chances.

10. The tearful woman told the judge that her father and his brother tried to gain control of the trust that was set up by her grandfather.

Syntax — ambiguity

The following sentences make ambiguous statements because of faulty word order. Revise each sentence with the quickest and simplest editing. Do not delete facts. Keep each sentence as a single sentence.

1. An unemployed nurse who advertised in a newspaper for a baby to adopt said Monday that she has been deluged by calls from dozens of people willing to give up their children, including the husband of a rape victim and several teen-agers.

2. The sister of slain Playmate Dorothy Stratten has filed a $5 million libel suit in Los Angeles against her stepfather and Playboy magazine founder Hugh Hefner.

3. Australian officials said all the animals have been replaced with funds donated by Australians and by outside sources.

4. White's appearance coincided with a voter registration booth at a shopping center.

5. A 30-year prison sentence was ordered Tuesday for a Brightsville resident who pleaded guilty to killing one of three employees of a pizza restaurant found slaind last year.

6. A Brightsville woman who will accompany the birds south said one was found almost frozen because of a cold snap by a woman downtown.

7. U.S. Ambassador Robert Strausz-Hupe went to Erzurum and announced that Washington was sending 1,000 tents, 156,000 blankets, 250 plastic sheets, 50 stoves, 50 gas cans, 2,000 water containers and two water pumps worth a total of $2 million.

8. Walsh said Tuesday that he will present evidence that links Toole with the death of 19-year-old Kevin McCarthy of Brightsville, whose bullet-riddled body was found in Central County after his car ran out of gas.

... **ambiguity**, continued

9. If ordered by the court, Autry's body will be taken to the Central County medical examiner for an autopsy before it is turned over to the family.

10. "We're going to stay here until we've talked to him or until there's nothing left to say," said Lois Robison, whose 17-year-old son awaits execution and who is a grade-school teacher in a Fort Worth suburb.

11. In 1974 Conrad began an association that lasted practically uninterrupted until his death when he became head clerk of the Offenbach Hotel.

12. It won't be real Texas chili unless you put your heart into it and leave out the beans.

13. The Brightsville Parks Board has passed an ordinance that outlaws cows grazing by the roadside and riding bicycles on the sidewalks.

14. Hundreds of schoolchildren had climbed the mountain with their teachers and rucksacks on their backs.

15. The governor wore a stickpin in his purple tie and shiny shoes.

16. Representatives from 14 Brightsville liquor stores met Wednesday night to hear advice about how to protect themselves from Police Chief Ambrose Bierce.

17. Nearby was the food table, presided over by Betty Parker, filled with delicious cakes.

18. The ship will stop for four hours. After taking on water and a brief walk around the city, the crew will hoist sail at midnight.

19. The body was found by a maid on a vacant lot next to the motel.

20. Authorities said Roberts was shot twice, once in the neck and in the back and leg.

Syntax — non sequiturs

A non sequitur is a literary construction that establishes a premise from which a logical inference does not follow. In news writing, non sequiturs usually appear as introductory phrases or clauses. News room wags like to recite the story about the reader who wrote the New York Times: "A native of Peoria, Ill., I am damned tired of your non sequiturs." Fix the following sentences to avoid the non sequiturs. The solution often is to subordinate one idea.

1. Born in Minnesota, Lochmond is the only person in Brightsville to see Halley's comet twice.

2. A graduate of Brightsville high school, Jeff Griffin attained the rank of captain in the Marine Corps.

3. A five-year veteran of the Navy, Bender, 28, won for his performance Saturday and Sunday in eight events, including the 20-foot rope climb.

4.The car was registered to a San Antonio man, although several residents of the Brightsville apartment project said they remembered seeing the car parked there before.

5. A resident of Utah, Johnson graduated fifth in a class of 800.

6. Built high on a hill, the house was painted black to absorb the heat.

7. Trained in Kentucky, the horse was sold to the owner of a stable in New Mexico.

8. A native of California, Smith lived in Brightsville a short time.

9. A student of Poe and other authors of Gothic stories, the professor found trout fishing to his liking.

10. Darting and ducking before the game, the spectators were entertained by seagulls.

Syntax — participial phrases

The unattached participial phrase, although condoned by many reporters and editors, is nevertheless ungrammatical—and unacceptable to newspapers with a high standard of desk work. (It should be no less acceptable in a company publication, a publicity release or a letter home.) The press of deadlines may not make it prudent to correct some unattached participial phrases, but, when time permits, a good copy editor will look for a way to make the sentence grammatical. Frequently, a conjunction and a finite verb will do the trick. For example:

> The victim told police that the two men knocked on her
> door about 10 p.m., saying they needed to make a phone
> call (..*and said they needed to make a phone call*).

If a long, involved sentence contains an unattached participial phrase, sometimes a correction may be made by constructing two sentences without hurting the flow of the story. Subordination is also a remedy. Examine each of the following sentences for unattached participial phrases and make corrections when appropriate.

1. Soto did not go back in the second inning, complaining of shoulder problems again.

2. Sutton relaxed in front of his locker, sorting through messages.

3. The writer finished the script just after midnight, beating the deadline by minutes.

4. The defendant drew a 25-year term, serving only 12 years.

5. Two planes collided over the Grand Canyon Wednesday, killing 25 crew and

passengers.

6. Cousteau emphasized that politics and ecology do not mix, maintaining that only a

mass movement can save the world environment from more deterioration.

7. The police chief said that not a single officer had been killed in the line of duty in five

years, urging the council not to interfere with departmental operating procedures.

8. The train rumbled down the tracks of the Goose Lake 55, the railroad saved by a

. . . participial phrases, continued

postmaster and a state lottery and named by a high school student, heading slowly south

through sparsely populated Modoc County in northeast California.

9. Wendell set the camera's timer on 10 seconds, enabling herself to be both photographer

and model, somehow yanking the TV onto her back.

10. A woman named George is a regular, singing *Johnny Has Herpes* and usually getting

the crowd to join in.

11. The captain put down the glass of beer, smacking his lips and making a gurgling noise.

12. Like Judy, Mike talks about enrolling in school, adding that he hopes to return by fall.

13. Jennifer's problems began in the first grade, giving her an instant dislike of school.

14. The assailant cried wildly, beating his chest and stamping his feet.

15. The ceremony will be held tomorrow, honoring those who have given their lives for

their country.

16. Total precipitation for the 24 hours ending at 7 p.m. was 2 inches, missing by .01 of

an inch the amount that had fallen by this time last year.

17. The child sat alone in the sand under the tree, playing with rocks, clods and sticks.

18. The gunman fired a volley of shots, killing a deputy before dying of his wounds

19. The president's aides argued forcefully against an invasion, insisting that the United

States had more to lose than to gain by such an action.

20. The corporal reported to the company commander, coming to attention and saluting

snappily as he entered the room.

Syntax —dangling modifiers

Searching for another subdivision of syntax, an idea burst upon us: You need something on dangling modifiers. Care will be required, of course; being sophisticated, a grammar trick would never get past readers of this book. Thinking of ways to offset this, a scheme took shape, calling for examples from regular reading.

Usually less contrived than the sentences above, we see a lot of dangling participles in newspapers. Produced unwittingly, you will find many examples of almost ludicrous phrasing in newspapers. Written in total seriousness, many reporters do stories that provide great pleasure to word watchers. Unable to sustain this thin joke any longer, will you let us switch to a straighter approach? You surely recognize dangling modifiers by now.

Most writers know better than to dangle a modifier, but they get in a hurry. Take your time. Edit the following sentences to undangle any modifiers.

1. Although he was hailed as a hero when he returned from his first voyage, the teacher

said Columbus faced growing skepticism when he failed to return with the gold and silks

of the Far East.

2. Faced with a leveling off of the economy and reductions in sales tax revenue, the

outlook for the next fiscal year for the city was described as grim.

3. Led by Chief Justice William Rehnquist, a ruling Thursday by the U.S. Supreme Court

held that workers may file sexual harassment suits under federal civil rights law.

4. Walking into Panama Jack's, an array of shirts, jeans and sunscreen greets the eye.

5. Addressing a high school commencement in the New Jersey town where President

Johnson and Alexei Kosygin, then the Soviet premier, met in 1967, the president's speech

noted that in recent months a potentially positive atmosphere had developed.

... dangling modifiers, continued

6. Hearing tearful testimony from a mother in her son's behalf, the court's decision was to show mercy.

7. Plunging down the deep ravine, the driver of the sports car escaped with only scratches.

8. Walking down the street, the child's pet followed him.

9. Rejecting the argument by the developer, the session was adjourned by the chairman of the commission.

10. Rolling across the porch, the girl lost the quarter as it disappeared into a crack.

11. Available in customizing kits, a good do-it-yourselfer can assemble the solarium in 12 hours.

12. Hampered by a chronic foot injury, a doctor advised him to give up basketball.

13. Smelly, dank and noisy, the reporters hurried past the pig pens.

14. Entitled, "Is This World Doomed to Ruin?" the speaker scripturally proves that the future of the planet Earth is bright.

15. Graduating from the University of Colorado with a degree in pharmacy, her flying career began in 1979.

. . . danging modifiers, continued

16. As a freshman at SU at Brookings this season, the upgrading of women's sports was witnessed firsthand by the Huron High graduate.

17. Once cooked, they topped the bread with assorted seasonings.

18. While driving along Highway 404, the community seems more like a resort hotel.

19. Being a nonsmoker, his lungs had to adjust.

20. The most highly recruited basketball player in the history of Orange County, Jova's services are coveted by all major schools.

21. After owning the vehicle four months, Bibby said, the transmission began to leak.

22. Like any other bird farmer, the noise is music to his ears.

23. Rushing in the door after a busy day at school, a youngster's first thought is often an after-school snack.

24. The ship is a bit dusty from its trip to the city, but after a good bath and some minor repairs, Gruber plans to exhibit her.

25. Once moved to the Williams home, the Burkett employees reassembled the tank.

Spelling

Your name _____

Date _____

Here are some of the most commonly misspelled words in news writing. Circle the correct spelling or *don't know* when appropriate. At least one can be spelled two ways, because the spellings refer to different words. Circle both correct spellings in such cases.

1.	accessible	accessable	don't know
2.	accidently	accidentally	don't know
3.	grammer	grammar	don't know
4.	Carribean	Caribbean	don't know
5.	accommodate	acommodate	don't know
6.	arguement	argument	don't know
7.	anoint	annoint	don't know
8.	definately	definitely	don't know
9.	developement	development	don't know
10.	existence	existance	don't know
11.	pronounciation	pronunciation	don't know
12.	occasion	occassion	don't know
13.	privilege	priviledge	don't know
14.	dependant	dependent	don't know
15.	irresistible	irresistable	don't know
16.	consensus	concensus	don't know
17.	occurrence	ocurrence	don't know
18.	concience	conscience	don't know
19.	committment	commitment	don't know
20.	embarrass	embarass	don't know
21.	indispensible	indispensable	don't know
22.	allotted	alotted	don't know
23.	dilettante	dilletante	don't know
24.	liason	liaison	don't know
25.	batallion	battalion	don't know
26.	connoiseur	connoisseur	don't know
27.	precede	preceed	don't know
28.	ecstasy	estasy	don't know
29.	vacuum	vaccuum	don't know
30.	nickel	nickle	don't know
31.	tyrannous	tyranous	don't know
32.	drunkeness	drunkenness	don't know
33.	forego	forgo	don't know
34.	sacreligious	sacrilegious	don't know
35.	prerogative	perogative	don't know
36.	iridescent	irridescent	don't know
37.	inadvertent	inadvertant	don't know
38.	geneology	genealogy	don't know
39.	villify	vilify	don't know
40.	innoculate	inoculate	don't know
41.	innocuous	inocuous	don't know
42.	superintendent	superintendant	don't know
43.	all right	alright	don't know
44.	admissable	admissible	don't know
45.	appalled	appaled	don't know
46.	arctic	artic	don't know
47.	benefitted	benefited	don't know

Date _____

48.	cemetery	cemetary	don't know
49.	changeable	changable	don't know
50.	noticable	noticeable	don't know
51.	deductible	deductable	don't know
52.	defendant	defendent	don't know
53.	protestor	protester	don't know
54.	eighth	eigth	don't know
55.	familiar	familar	don't know
56.	similar	similiar	don't know
57.	gauge	gage	don't know
58.	guerilla	guerrilla	don't know
59.	auxiliary	auxilary	don't know
60.	hanger	hangar	don't know
61.	hemorrhage	hemorahage	don't know
62.	judgeship	judgship	don't know
63.	laboratory	labortory	don't know
64.	irrelevant	irrevelant	don't know
65.	lightning	lightening	don't know
66.	questionnaire	questionaire	don't know
67.	likable	likeable	don't know
68.	maintainance	maintenance	don't know
69.	managable	manageable	don't know
70.	ninety	ninty	don't know
71.	niece	neice	don't know
72.	pari-mutuel	pari-mutual	don't know
73.	persevere	persavere	don't know
74.	penicillin	pencilin	don't know
75.	Philipines	Philippines	don't know
76.	phenomenon	phenomeon	don't know
77.	personnel	personel	don't know
78.	recommend	reccommend	don't know
79.	receive	recieve	don't know
80.	interfered	interferred	don't know
81.	transfered	transferred	don't know
82.	recognizance	recognisance	don't know
83.	reconnaissance	reconaissance	don't know
84.	renaissance	rennaissance	don't know
85.	salable	saleable	don't know
86.	miniscle	minuscule	don't know
87.	separate	saparate	don't know
88.	sergeant	sargeant	don't know
89.	sizeable	sizable	don't know
90.	supprise	surprise	don't know
91.	skilfull	skillful	don't know
92.	truely	truly	don't know
93.	villian	villain	don't know
94.	wierd	weird	don't know
95.	weild	wield	don't know
96.	beseige	besiege	don't know
97.	yeild	yield	don't know
98.	wilful	willful	don't know
99.	untill	until	don't know
100.	materiel	matarial	don't know

Your name _____

Attribution — Exercise 1

Date _____

Examine the attributive verbs in the following sentences and supply more suitable verbs if appropriate.

1. "It's pay now or pay later," the mechanic grinned.

2. "Shut up," he explained.

3. The Democratic candidate pointed out that his opponent was inarticulate and unwise.

4. "A victory Saturday will be the high point of my career," the coach exclaimed.

5. The banker admitted that the vault had not been secured the night before the robbery.

6. Residents have been asked to use water only for sanitary purposes in order to allow the

drained reservoirs to fill, the engineer commented.

7. "We pride ourselves on being an open board," the chairman noted.

8. "Place the dynamite in a cool place and don't drop it," the expert emphasized.

9. Approval of the liquor permit would be harmful to the church, the mayor pointed out.

10. "We can do it," the coach told the team. "We can do it," the team echoed.

11. "We must give aid to the contras or be known as a friend that can't be trusted," the

president urged.

12. "This is one jury that's stacked," the courhouse wag opined.

... **exercise 1,** continued

13. "Kill the bastards," the sergeant cried.

14. "Only a brain-damaged person would make such a request," the chief of staff asserted.

15. "The play is just too boring," the critic yawned.

16. "We are in a preliminary discussion with Six Flags and the state regarding a 150-acre theme park on the state Hog Farm," summed up Robert Foster, head of commercial development.

17. "And finally let me say that the richest person in the world is the one with the most money," the speaker concluded.

18. A snake with a long, narrow head and slit eyes will not harm you, the zoo keeper reassured the visitors. "But it may scare the life out of you," he added.

19. "Take my life but don't take my money," the senator thundered in opposing the appropriation bill during floor debate. A colleague nearby nodded. "He really means it," the colleague smiled.

20. His voice heavy with sarcasm, the teacher added that two and two make four.

Attribution — Exercise 2

Edit these sentences. Do not worry about problems other than attribution and style. You do not need to make connections between any of the items, because they do not make up a story. Unless otherwise specified, all statements are attributable to Dr. Bailey Marshall, director of the High School Athletic League, but they are not quotations unless they have quotation marks. Beware of excessive attribution. Got that? OK, a little attribution music, please.

1. Betty Apson, director of Megastate University's Division of Recreational Sports, has been appointed to serve on the High School Athletic League's State Executive Committee, HSAL Director Bailey Marshall announced today.

2. Thompson has a Master of Arts degree in physical education from Ohio State University, Dr. Marshall said. Thompson said in an interview that she taught at Ohio State four years before joining the MU faculty.

3. Dr. Emette S. Redford will retire March 30 after 37 years' service on the HSAL state Executive Committee, HSAL Director Bailey Marshall said Friday. Redford has been a strong force in the league's development, Marshall said.

4. High School Athletic League schools voted to move the girls' volleyball program to the fall by a vote of 682 to 286, according to Dr. Bailey Marshall, HSAL director. The change should produce a marked increase in the number of Class A schools participating and a decrease in B schools participating.

... **exercise 2,** continued

5. (Marshall talking.) "One of the problems we have had in the past is that we've been a

narrow fund. We had only 1,000 contributors last year. I hope to broaden our support."

6. Ten members will be elected to the HSAL Legislative Council this year, UIL Director

Bailey Marshall announced Wednesday. Four of them will replace retiring members.

7. (Marshall talking.) "The sign is here. It's just a matter of what words they put on it."

8. (Mayor's quotes.) The mayor asked about the bridge. "I need to know the cost now,

because we may have to scrap the whole project. I'd hate that."

9. Brightsville is in for a nasty weekend, forecasters at the National Weather Service

believe. A cold front will hit tonight, they declared.

10. Another frost has hit the Brazilian coffee crop, and a new increase in prices is

expected, Brazilian authorities say.

Attribution — Exercise 3

Attribution is required in a news story when statements are subjective, highly charged or controversial. Attribution is also a device to establish the authority for a story—that is, to tell the reader the source of the information.

Obviously, not every statement requires attribution. You have three tasks in this next exercise:

1. Decide whether to use attribution. 2. Having decided to use attribution, choose the proper place for it. 3. Choose the proper form, in particular the right verb.

When attribution is used to establish the authority for the story, the attribution often fits more smoothly in the second paragraph than in the first. Examine the attribution in the following examples and use the attribution in the second paragraph instead of the lead when appropriate. Keep in mind that attribution is often used in the lead to give timeliness to a story that would otherwise be stale by news standards. By writing, ". . . an official said Thursday," the reporter imparts immediacy to an event that happened or took place Wednesday—or earlier.

Laboratory tests determined Wednesday that a second death was caused by cyanide-laced Extra-Strength Excedrin capsules, law enforcement officials said.

The possibility was raised that other cyanide deaths would be discovered.

* * *

WASHINGTON--The space agency abruptly abandoned Thursday a $700 million program to use the space shuttle for launching Centaur rockets that would propel scientific probes to Jupiter and the sun, it was announced by NASA Administrator James Fletcher.

The agency will examine other alternatives for the planetary and scientific payloads scheduled to use the liquid-fueled Centaur upper stage, Fletcher said.

* * *

... **exercise 3,** continued

CHICAGO--Last month was one of the city's worst months ever for robberies, which

showed an 80 percent increase from the same month a year ago, police said.

Monthly statistics announced Tuesday also showed the number of car thefts was nearly

71 percent greater than last year at this time, police said.

* * *

A spectator went berserk in a crowded Brightsville courtroom today, pulled a gun and

wounded 12 people on a bloody mission that was revealed to him during a vision, police

said he told them after he was subdued.

The gunman, Anthony Armstrong, is being held under guard in a psychiatric unit after

the 11 a.m. rampage in the courtroom of General Sessions Judge Jerome Obermark.

* * *

SAN YSIDRO--Biologists conducting an inventory of plant and animal life in Paraguay

have found species entirely new to science, researchers in that South American nation say.

The biologists have also discovered the existence of the northern anaconda, a snake that

can grow to 15 feet and 150 pounds.

MANILA--Rescue workers recovered three more bodies Tuesday from a two-story

textile factory that collapsed Sunday, police said.

The death toll now stands at 14. Three factory officials have been charged with

negligence.

* * *

A city jail prisoner escaped today after his cellmate let him take his place when it was

time for the cellmate to be released, police said.

The prisoner who remained behind—Gregg Randall, 23—has been charged with aiding

an escape. He was jailed in connection with traffic charges. He is still in jail.

* * *

The First National Bank was robbed Monday by three men who fled with $100,000 in

marked money, police said.

The men fled in a maroon Nissan Pulsar NX and were last seen going south on West

First Street.

* * *

Attribution — Exercise 4

Delete unnecessary attribution in the following story where inappropriate. The story is supported by photocopies of the pertinent documents.

A going-away dinner for a former councilman cost Ocala taxpayers more than

$1,000, according to records in the city treasurer's office.

The dinner for the former councilman, Howell Graham, was held at the Embers, said

Treasurer Lynn Rockwell. Rockwell said the dinner was one of several high-dollar

expenses that the City Council and staff have charged on city credit cards in the past year.

Mayor Mike McDee defended the dinner on the ground that Graham had served without

pay. McDee said that during Graham's more than six years on the council that members

served without pay. Only since 1986 have councilmen received $300 a month, he said.

The mayor said the dinner expense was justified but he did not attend. The event

attracted 30 persons, including councilmen and their spouses and city staff members and

their spouses, the mayor said.

The billing statements in city vouchers show the date of the expense, the location and

the amount, the treasurer said. The statements do not indicate the nature of business or

who attended, the treasurer said.

... **exercise 4,** continued

The mayor said there is no abuse of the credit cards issued by the city, but he said he would be concerned if thousands of dollars in expenses cannot be substantiated.

The mayor said that if credit cards were abused the city would "certainly take a much harsher approach" toward accountability.

All the mayor's $1,600 in expenses during this fiscal year lack receipts other than the statement from the credit card company, the city treasurer said. The mayor said the billing statements are receipt enough, but the treasurer disagreed.

"I've always wanted a more stringent system of accountability," the treasurer said. "I don't like paying any bills without receipts."

The MasterCards that the city uses are issued to all councilmen and are available to certain department heads, the treasurer said.

The City Council is using a relatively new system for expenses, Mayor McDee said. Before this year, when city business was discussed during lunch or dinner, the meal would be an out-of-pocket expense for the councilmen, McDee said.

Attribution — Exercise 5

Overattribution clutters a direct quotation, distracts the reader and wastes space. The following excerpts from stories have double, triple or even quadruple attribution. Keep the quotations but cut the attributions to a more acceptable number.

"It's rather cool here," he commented as he strolled around the park. "What type of winter is this?

"I've been in Columbia twice before," he said. "I came here in 1980 and was back in 1984. I was in the Army then," he laughed. "The first time I was on a recruiting trip.

"Then in the fall of '84 I was on the way to Kansas City and stayed overnight en route," he recalled.

* * *

"It's obviously the way we should go," Hankins said. "It would eliminate duplication of government, duplication of service.

"As far as services go, we have two governments, two mayors and two school boards," Hankins said. "The mayor of Columbia appoints certain people, and the county judge appoints certain people. There's a duplication.

"If there was one board in control, things could be a lot more efficient," he said.

* * *

The commission issued a report that said, "The number of women on the faculty is so

small that while the women are almost invisible within the campus community, they are so

visible to each other as to be constantly reminded of their isolation.

"In large part they attribute their small numbers to the university's apparent token

concern with affirmative action," the report said.

* * *

"The problem of a shortage of women in high positions is not any more severe at

Central Community College than anywhere else," Costello said.

"If you looked at Duke or Emory you would see the same thing," she said.

* * *

"The union wanted to be downtown because it felt it would help its identity, aid its

recruiting and help in its determination to be a good corporate citizen," Wurf said.

"Brightsville was chosen after studies also of Cincinnati, St. Louis and Louisville," he

added.

* * *

... **exercise 5,** continued

"I missed that first putt and should have had it," Hogan said. "Then I really messed up

my tee shot. But I came back as best I could.

"I'm sorry that Jones didn't qualify," Hogan said.

* * *

"The Masters has long been a prestigious tournament, dating back to 1951," said Ed

Baur, the tournament manager. "This is one event that every sports fan should plan to

see," Baur said.

* * *

"In the AIC meet I did six events," Culp said. "I think that bothered me in the hurdles.

I think I was just tired after two days. I wanted to beat Allen. We had a pretty good race.

"I know I could do better," he said.

* * *

The Trapper, blessed with the eye of an eagle and the mind of a highly sophisticated

computer, replied: "I'm going with 'almost 30,000.' I consulted with a policeman

... exercise 5, continued

experienced in counting people and a longtime official of the annual racing event before

coming up with that figure. It was not easy to estimate how many people were there," he

added.

* * *

Young recalled one case with obvious regret. "We had a sheet metal apprentice in our

program who came through the class at Central High," he said. "He was a national champ.

"He went to his employer and said, 'You either give me what I want or I'm gone.' The

employer let him go, and he ended up working at a hamburger joint," Young said.

Attribution — Exercise 6

A qualified statement allows a reporter to introduce a valid idea into a story without having to cite a source. Obviously, this requires care. A story may say the president *appeared* angry or disgruntled, because the reporters do not know when behavior is an act and when it is not. The reporter often does better by describing the action and letting the reader make an inference: *The president shouted at an aide, kicked the wastebasket and slammed the door.* Otherwise, careful reporting requires the qualified generalization. Qualifying a statement can also retain its mood, which may be lost or damaged by attribution. For example:

Attributed: The fire was a result of arson, police said.
Qualified: The fire was blamed on arson.

If we used the second version of the statement, we no doubt would attribute that information to the police in the second or third paragraph.

Qualify the following sentences. Keep editing to a minimum in the revisions. Do not qualify with the words *may* or *might.* Bear in mind, too, that simple statements of easily verifiable fact can be left unqualified. You recall the one from the text: *The moon is 186,000 miles from Earth, according to the Associated Press.* Actually, the distance varies a little. But you get the point. When in doubt, qualify. Just don't go overboard.

1. Monday's high temperature was only a preview of what is in store for Brightsville this

week. Readings of 100 or more will turn the city into a humid oven until cool air pours

into the area next Monday.

2. The third man from the right in the police lineup was nervous.

3. The meeting will be at 7 p.m. Friday in the Municipal Auditorium.

4. The mayor broke his campaign promise to seek lower taxes and encourage park

development.

5. The actress regretted having to cancel the performance and return to California.

... **exercise 6,** continued

6. The water commissioner wants to develop water districts in rural areas, which can then

be opened for development.

7. A single protester fired up the crowd, which then turned into a mob.

8. Their slow death in the flames that consumed the high rise hotel was the most horrible

death imaginable.

9. The stabbing was a result of a long-simmering feud between the two pool shooters.

10. If the United States makes a heavy arms commitment to the contras in Nicaragua, it is

certain that a Vietnam kind of quagmire will develop.

11. The day will not soon return when investors can get interest rates like those of the late

'70s.

12. The robber was wearing a fully buttoned double-breasted coat, and the outline of a gun

could be seen at his waist.

13. The assailant's hair had been dyed because the roots were lighter than the rest of the

hair.

14. The crowd watching the parade was the largest in the town's history.

. . . **exercise 6,** continued

15. A terrorist organization named Dacoit is the group responsible for the piracy of a cruise ship and the deaths of six passengers.

16. The celebration scheduled July 4 will attract more than 10,000 people.

17. Snow is now falling throughout the state, and by morning accumulations will be up to 14 inches.

18. The Mississippi has risen 14 feet in the last three days, and residents downstream are stacking sandbags to turn back the water when the river reaches them tomorrow with a crest 4 feet above flood stage.

19. The president had trouble answering questions during the press conference.

20. The nurse was calm and composed—even cheerful—when she was arrested in the deaths of seven infants, all of whom died of over medication while they were under her care.

Attribution — Exercise 7

Attribution is said to be overextended when the reporter embellishes a source's idea or statement with an idea that did not come from the source. For example:

> The state controller announced Monday that oil revenue decreased 35 percent in the first quarter, *a sign that the worst economic crisis in the state's history is just around the corner.*

The ideas in bold face in the examples below were supplied by the reporter, not the source. The remedy usually is a period and a new sentence backed by the proper authority. Sometimes you simply eliminate the judgmental word.   Provide an appropriate remedy for the overextended attribution in the following examples.

1. The chairman said the airline had also talked to People Express about buying some of

the assets of the **financially troubled** airline.

2. The chairman said changing industry conditions complicate equipment purchasing

decisions, **another reason that it pays airlines to be wary of bargain hunting.**

3. Glass said $25,000 had been spent on development of the test kit, **which will**

include at least 96 tests and give ranchers an option that has not been

available before.

4. Cardinal Miguel Obando y Bravo on Sunday mourned the forced closing of La Prensa,

Nicaragua's opposition newspaper. Obando said the government should reflect on the

... **exercise 7,** continued

recently toughened position against moderate dissenting voices in the press.

5. **The disease has struck the community in epidemic proportions and taken a toll of lives uncommon even in that part of New Mexico,** which is responding to the problem with increased medical aid, the governor said.

6. The International Monetary conference announced Tuesday that 200 international bankers and government officials will meet in Boston next week for three days of shop talk **at a time of increasing friction among the world's industrialized nations over international trade.**

7. The Commerce Department said Friday that the nation's foreign trade deficit narrowed to $12.1 billion last month from $14.5 billion the previous month, **though analysts were divided on whether the decline represented a turning point for the nation's trade troubles.**

8. "We're not concerned about Sears, per se, owning a bank," said a Federal Reserve official who asked not to be identified. "We're concerned when a lot of little companies own banks and own them simply to get access to unlimited credit," **which can lead to foreclosures that leave the government holding the bag.**

... **exercise 7,** continued

9. The union president said the work week dropped from 69 hours in 1870 to 40 hours in

1940, **when the 30-hour work week probably was not even an embryonic**

thought.

10. A quarter of U.S. households were touched by crimes involving violence or theft last

year, **a clear indication that the massive move of people to urban areas has**

made crime a statistical fact of life for more than 60 million Americans, the

Justice Department announced Sunday.

Attribution — Exercise 8

Make appropriate corrections in the following passages, which include material quoted directly. Not all the errors are in the quotations. The items are not related. Note that No. 7 has three paragraphs; they form a long unit.

1. "Then 20 seconds later there was another burst of machine-gun fire, Smith said.

"There was great confusion. . . . Soldiers were running backward and forward."

2. "Despite the best efforts by a team of doctors . . . she could not be saved," the hospital

medical superintendent said.

3. Speaker Wright dismissed the wave that swept Reagan to a second term. He said it

was not a mandate for his conservative agenda, but proved instead that he is "a great TV

manipulator. He is a very popular man. But the voters sent Democrats to Congress."

4. House Minority Leader Robert H. Michel of Illinois said that "people shouldn't expect

too many victories."

5. The councilman said a schedule was needed for the drafting and enactment of a new

comprehensive plan because of "the hopelessly frantic pace of Brightsville development.

6. "I've heard people say: "My God, if they do that to us, they'll do it to everyone."

7. "I'm not suggesting there's any direct quid pro quo," Cox said. But anyone testifying

before such a committee on a bill backed or opposed by his campaign contributors "would

feel that he didn't get a fair shot at it or that he was rooked out of it entirely.

"And I'm not suggesting but asserting it's all too likely, as many members of Congress

have said, that members of the committee, in casting their votes, are bound to worry about

contributions when it comes to the next campaign."

"We would all like to join forces in working for fair and clean campaigns," said Felix

McIntyre, the independent candidate in the race.

That was a pretty short exercise. Let's do some more on the same assignment. Good quotations do not rely on parenthetical material to explain them. With few exceptions, it is more effective to paraphrase direct quotations than to prop them up with parenthetical explanations, as done in the following examples. Paraphrase the following to make indirect quotations when appropriate. If you keep the parenthetical material, be sure punctuation is correct.

1. "They (the state commission) can do it, but they don't do it often."

2. "I'm appalled that it (the recommendation to close the library) has made it this far," the

teacher said.

3. "I think he (Reagan) is going to win—and win big," Bush said.

4. "Right now all the other (death row) cases probably would come under the same kind

of grounds for a stay," the warden said.

5. "Really, the only way to prevent it (hepatitis) is to wash your hands before you eat and

after you go to the bathroom, and I mean every time," said the health service official.

6. "We wish to express our objections and outrage at the action of the department's employees who staked out adult-oriented establishments (and) took license plate numbers of individuals who were not engaged in any form of illegal activity . . ." said a letter from the president of the American Civil Liberties Union.

7. "I entered CU with 35 hours (of credit) and was able to graduate in three years, plus I didn't have to sit through courses I already had," she said.

8. "It hurt all of us. It hurt (former precinct commissioner) John Milloy way back there. It hurt (County Judge Mike) Renfro. It would have hurt (Precinct 2 Commissioner Bob) Honts if he had run, and obviously it hurt me," Moya said.

9. "Sometimes I feel that every loser and dropout who wants a dodge calls himself an artist. But at the same time (the artistic community) has a small percentage of the best, most interesting people within the culture."

10. "The quality of the water (determines) in large measure the quality of life . . . (and) man can save or destroy life," he said.

11. "He has (managed to) increase fishing and at the same time increase the stock," Key said. "No other country does this."

12. "My friend gave (the four bills) to my brother to play the video machine," the youth

told the police.

13. "They couldn't own a piece of land, but they could bring their own merchandise and

sell it in a store. (Retailing) was the easiest way to do it."

14. "I've even got (a needle) for my putting stroke," he said.

15. The commissioner said, "Had the people in the northern part of the county voted for it,

they would have offset the small (losing margin) in the south."

16. "We feel like (the current EPA restriction) is a little severe or strict."

17. "He also tried to slap me in the (groin). I don't know the guy but I can tell you this. I

don't like him."

18. "The team wanted to present the gift (to the coach) after dinner so everyone could see."

19. The affidavit said ". . .we were walking (down the boardwalk) when the officer

approached us (from across the street). Then we heard shots and the officer fell."

20. "Tim (the shopkeeper) was always there when we needed him. I mean if the item was

hard to get, we could count on Tim to find one."

Attribution — Exercise 9

When a word or a phrase is quoted, it creates a fragmentary or orphan quote. In the following sentences, delete the quotation marks when the quoted word or phrase is used in the ordinary sense and the quotation marks are not justified. If you come across a slang term, either change it to a normal word or drop the quotation marks and use it without apology.

1. The astronauts were given the "key" to the city in a ceremony at the City Hall.

2. The actress gave an "incandescent" performance.

3. The man arrested at the border told customs officials he was an "importer."

4. The agriculture commissioner said the state "should be in a position of supporting the goals of the lawsuit ."

5. The women said they are "fourth cousins" and Curtis was a distant uncle to them.

6. The TV announcer said he did not have the "foggiest" idea of what meteorology was all about.

7. For some, all they remember is being called a "baby killer" or "dope addict" when they returned home.

8. An American who was on the plane said the gunman seemed "desperate."

9. The Israeli said Waldheim was without doubt a "killer."

10. Reagan told those who oppose the arms buildup to "tell it to the Marines."

11. Before Sontaire dropped out he estimated he missed "20 or 30 days" of school.

12. The skipper said the boat was plain—with "no bells or whistles."

13. Stompfer said the debate in the House was a "joke" the way that it was being

conducted.

14. The cowboy had gained the respect of the entire ranch, but after the roundup he

decided it was time to "move on."

15. House Speaker Jim Wright said the Senate's committee members had "hornswoggled"

the representatives into voting for Dole's plan.

16. The work of those nuns helped many Catholics advance from "a true underclass" to

the ranks of affluent Americans, Murphy said.

17. The lawmaker said that members of the commission were "genuinely concerned with

high school dropouts" as they debated which measure to include in the House bill.

18. The journalism professor said the board would impose censorship "behind my dead

body."

19. The writing students set out to find a "horse of the same color."

20. The clerk said he lives in a two-bedroom "mansion" on the poor side of town.

21. The undertaker tentatively opened the coffin, and the "dead" man uttered a sound.

Quotation

Your name _____

Date _____

Quotation — Exercise 1

Some reporters develop a habit of using a direct quotation that says the same thing as the narrative preceding it. We call that material a stutter quote or echo quote. The remedy is not always as simple as killing the quotation, whose color and freshness of expression may warrant its retention. Make corrections in the following passages, which contain echo quotes. You may adjust the unquoted parts.

1. Nolan said he left college before graduation and joined the Highway Patrol because he could not pass freshman English. "Quite frankly, I could never master freshman English," he said.

2. When the commission, unable to decide on a solution, adjourned, County Executive Pat Williams urged commissioners to continue to study the problem, saying, "It's something we need to continue to work on."

3. Beyond the relief the program offers the inmates is the newfound and lasting feeling that they can deal with problems through running.

   "If I have a problem, I can deal with it a lot more easily if I run," an inmate said.

4. Principal William Brandon said the sixth-graders raise the flag each day, and they sometimes make mistakes. "Once in a while the flag gets stepped on, or they will let it drag on the ground," he said. "But they do it every day. Shoot, nobody's perfect."

5. The president told members of Congress not to mistake his mood on the measure to

raise taxes. He said he would veto any such measure that came to his desk. "I will veto a

tax bill as sure as God made little green apples," he said.

6. The governor said the water permit was issued even though the board had promised to

conduct hearings and to announce a decision before approving a permit. "They issued a

permit in spite of their saying they would not do so without prior notification and prior

hearings," the governor said at a press conference Friday.

7. The fact that the team is 2-0 is no surprise to Colonel Crawford Coach Dave Fray.

"I'm not at all surprised about that," Fray said when asked about the record.

8. The award surprised McWilliams. "I am totally surprised by this," he said.

9. The skipper said he might have done better had the wind not come up. "I would have

finished higher if the wind had stayed down," he said.

10. Coach Farfle said his team will regroup and try to make a fresh start next week. "We'll

get together and try to start over next week," he said.

Quotation — Exercise 2

Some editors insist that material quoted directly be verbatim, but others allow minor corrections in grammar or diction to avoid embarrassment to the person quoted. Good judgment is the rule when corrections are allowed. You would not want a backwoods mountain man to sound like a Harvard professor. On the other hand, general circulation publications, not to mention company publications, do not to want gutter language to fill the pages. A dilemma. So you get the chore of cleaning it up. Indicate what corrections you would make in the following quotations if corrections were allowed.

1. A sheriff: "The jailer took him to the shower and beat the shit out of him."

2. State official: "Me and some of my friends worked too hard for me to get this job back

for me to let some clowns mess it up."

3. Citizen: "I must of got too slow 'cause I passed the house and a guy hollered out and

cussed me. He asked me, 'What are you looking at, you dumb ol' bastard?'"

4. County official: "Based on projections, we should of had enough money."

5. City Council candidate: "I'm real satisfied."

6. English teacher: "If I was Chaucer I would have added a little more ribaldry to some

of the tales."

7. Candidate: "You feel good. The word gets back you're doing good."

8. College baseball coach: "As far as the streak, he does have seven in a row and I had

eight as a starter, but I didn't have any relief assignments like he did last year."

9. Prep tennis player: "I went out of town one week and Ron got real good."

10. High school baseball coach: "But winning that first one and the pitching situation is

what concerns me."

11. Social figure: "Istanbul was a different culture but it looked like I thought it would."

12. Council member: "The city doesn't owe Union Square nothing."

13. Commissioner: "You can see who is riding who."

14. CPA: "If there was one board in control, things would be a lot more efficient."

15. Football coach: "The Lord knows I feel like I've been on the battlefield all my life."

16. President of the United States: "The God damned reporters are hounding me to death."

17. President, again: "No sonofabitch in U.S. industry is going to tell us what to do on

trade–in imports and exports."

18. University president: "We don't consider scheduling teams on the West Coast or the

Northeast like we used to."

19. University president: "We've made some progress in appointing women to upper-level

positions, but not as much as we would have liked to have made."

20. Woman activist: "It takes a man of some courage—a man with balls—to stand on the

side of women in their struggle for equality."

Quotation — Exercise 3

Are you offended yet? Sorry. At some point in life you will have to decide how you handle strong words in material like the preceding. You will also have to deal with material that goes the other way: Instead of being coarse, it tilts to the side of fanciness. You saw some of this a few pages back, in a section on elegance. Now you get a load of it in quotes. Keep the pages of your publication free of overblown language like that in the following quotes. Delete the quotation marks and paraphrase the material, or go with a partial quotation. Use regular words no matter what you do.

1. "He is not eligible to secure employment with Gulf until he has reached 21 years of age," Elred said.

2. "We think it would be futile for teachers to request more salary funds this year because the board is in a zero increase posture," the superintendent said.

3. "Our elementary schools will have a module—perhaps multiple modules—designed to enhance peer group interaction skills," Williams said.

4. "This product has stimulative functions and is sure to favorably impact the city's fiscal stability," the city manager said.

5. "We were not micromanaging Grenada, intelligencewise, until about the time frame of May or June," the officer said.

6. "The starting time for the Fun Run Walk will be approximately 15 minutes prior to the beginning of the other races," the official said.

7. "In this kind of situation, it is necessary that a community institution act in a leadership

. . . **exercise 3,** continued

role for initiating and facilitating the program," she said.

8. "The city of Brightsville has made inquiries into the possibility of expanding facilities

at the grain elevator in order to provide us the capacity to handle entire grain trains at once,"

the operator said.

9. "Naturally at this point and time I oppose the new school, and I oppose it pure and

simple because we do not have adequate funds to properly build the facilities to house

4,000 additional students," said Board of Education Chairman Tom Mullen, who is

running for re-election.

10. "It has not been necessary for the county to expend tax monies for hospital operation

during the decade just completed," the hospital administrator said.

11. "I thought we were in trouble in the second half, but we reeled off 12 unanswered

points, mainly by capitalizing on fast break opportunities, and pulled the fat out of the fire,"

the happy coach said.

Quotation — a quiz

Edit the following stories for style, grammar, diction, and spelling and all the aspects of quotation marks covered in the preceding exercises. Use appropriate editing symbols.

The new commander of the national guard has ordered his men to shave their beards. Men in his command must meet the "same standards of smartness" as those in the regular branches of the United States military service, he said.

General Tom Petty, who took over the guard August 30, sent out an urgent all-points directive Sun. night announcing the new regulation effective next Monday. The directive said: "I desire our military personnel to present a neat and professional appearance in keeping with longstanding military tradition. . . ."

"All guardsmen will be cleanshaven with the exception of neatly-trimmed and military-appearing mustaches," General Petty's directive said.

The order was not greeted enthusiastically in Honduras, where guardsmen are on maneuvers. Most of them have not shaved since arrive in Tegucigalpa three weeks ago.

"I think it (the order to shave) stinks," said Sergeant John Rowan of Killeen, Texas.

"We don't have much choice but to shave," said Pfc. Arnold Toynbee of New Orleans, La. "This guy's your boss. You do what he says."

* * *

Mass arrests within hours of a not-guilty verdict by an all-white jury in a police shooting

case was pivotal in preventing a major racial disturbance last week, officials said Sunday.

Brightsville and Central County police officials said almost 80 per cent of the more than

310 people arrested since the acquattal of police Officer Alvarez Thompson was

apprehended in the first 8 hours. Thompson was charged with accidental homocide in the

shooting death of a black man.

Raymond Long, Brightsville police spokesperson, said after the mass arrests there were

not many left to round up.

"There weren't many left to arrest," Long said. "We got large numbers of trouble-

makers off the street," Long said. "Those who were released didn't see any fun in being

arrested a second time," he said.

On Sunday, officers remained on the perimeters of problem neighborhoods, but Mariam

Glick, a spokesperson for Central County, said the number of officers was gradually being

reduced. Street barricades were removed Saturday.

"It's very quiet, extremely quiet," Glick said. "We're going back to normal working

...quiz, continued

conditions little by little." She said the department hoped to return to 8-hour shifts today.

* * *

A state district court jury handed down a 10-year probated sentence and A $10,000 fine

for B.W. Neeley Thursday for vehicular homicide.

The 4-man, 8-woman jury deliberated seven hours before reaching a "guilty" verdict late

Wednesday

The jury convicted Neeley Tuesday of killing his wife by driving his pickup into a utility

pole at a speed of 45 miles per hour. Mrs. Neeley died twenty minutes afterward from

internal injuries at Brightsville Hospital, where she was rushed by Media Ambulance.

The three Neeley children, Tom, Doris and Leroy, were injured but did not require

hospitalization. The accident occurred last November 11 on Old Dutchman Rd.

The state attorney asked that Neeley be "sent to jail for at least 50 years," but the jury

apparently were influenced by what the defense attorney described as "justifiable

response." Several witnesses for the defense testified they had seen Mrs. Neeley on more

than one occasion at nightclubs with different men.

The judge allowed the testimony over the objections of the state's attorney.

McNeeley said he thought he had "received a fair trial.

"I did wrong and I know I must pay the consequences," McNeeley said. "I acted in a fit

of rage, I'm just glad that I will still be able to take care of my kids. They seem to

understand," McNeeley said.

State's Atty. Tom Staykempt said the sentence was absurd due to the fact that McNeeley

is a cold-blooded killer who deserves to rot in prison and burn in hell.

"Neither Brightsville or Central County can afford to allow a murderer to get off with a

fine and probation," the prosecutor said.

State district court judge Tab Minor who presided at the 8-day trial could not be reached

for comment.

Clutter

Your name _____

Date _____

Clutter — a long exercise

Any word or words that do not contribute to the meaning or understanding of a sentence can be called clutter. Clutter may appear as redundancy or repetition. It may appear as officialese—the use of indirect and roundabout language. Clutter can also result from affectations that reporters and sources sometimes adopt in the mistaken belief that it emphasizes the importance of what they have to say. Basically, clutter is present if the ideas expressed go without saying, if the ideas are repetitive, or if the ideas are not expressed in the most direct way. However, this does not mean you have a license to strip every sentence bare. In dealing with clutter, you must avoid destroying the mood of a sentence. A good editor will maintain the reporter's writing style while guarding against damaging the flow of the words. Delete the clutter from the following sentences —whether just a word or a long phrase—as appropriate. Fix any other errors you run across, too.

1. City officials have decided not to fight the display of six giant dancing frogs that revolve atop the rooftop of a popular Dallas nightclub.

2. The Del Valle policy specifies that students should receive no more than three swats, and that swats should be given only by an administrator.

3. The San Antonio Performing Arts Association won the cultural organization award for arranging the world premier performance of the ballet *Jamboree.*

4. The Reagan administration, claiming that UNESCO is plagued by mismanagement and hostility to Western values, confirmed Wednesday that it was withdrawing from the 161-member body as of Dec. 31.

5. The task force asked the city staff to prepare a report for its meeting next week with information about all publicly owned land within the city boundaries.

6. The water control improvement district proposed by Carpenter and associates would

be located on mostly undeveloped land north of U.S. 290 at the intersection of Thomas

Springs and Stewart roads.

7. Sinkin said he was forced out as director of the Nuclear Information and Resource

Service after an internal organizational dispute.

8. Sinkin said he is undecided about his future plans.

9. Her benefactor, A.G. Shalda, died last month of head injuries and a fractured skull.

10. The officer said he signaled the youth to stop his car, but the youth continued driving.

11. Stevert said authorities are involved in an on-going investigation of the drug case.

12. Hickerson plans to serve a large area of land between Fayette and the interstate.

13. Threats have been made in Beirut by Moslem extremists vowing to attack anyone who

participated in the talks.

14. City officials have opened negotiations with Tex-Mex Railroad executives to reinstate

passenger train service between the coast and the border within the next two years.

15. The new city hall will replace the existing one between Eighth and Colorado streets.

16. The company is accused of destroying results of tests that did not accurately measure

leaks in the Unit 2 cooling system and of intentionally manipulating the leak test results by

adding water and hydrogen.

17. In Madrid, the U.S. currency hit a new record 155 pesetas, breaking the previous

record of 154.1 reached Friday.

18. John Ford, the assistant agriculture secretary, ordered a full-scale investigation of the

condition of the 21.5 million bushels of corn.

19. The victim was honored with a tribute in the school yearbook.

20. The council voted against a proposal to open city pools before the end of school.

21. Eleven-year-old twins were critically injured Tuesday when their mother's car was hit

head-on by another car that went out of control on an East St. Louis street.

22. If a tip isn't left on the table, he takes an additional 10 percent of the check and gives it

to the waitress.

23. The association is considering what alternatives it has, if any.

24. After years of work, and in an action that was hardly noticed in the chaos of

adjournment, Congress this week completed a broad, significant and controversial overhaul

of the federal criminal justice system.

25. Inspectors for the Department of Health searched Friday near Graham for a missing

thumb sized cylinder containing a highly radioactive material.

26. The bill essentially would put teeth in a non-binding trade resolution that was adopted

by the Senate Thursday on a unanimous 92-0 vote.

27. Ethiopian farmers face a critical seed shortage that must be resolved within three weeks

if the drought-plagued country is to grow food this year.

28. In Washington, the State Department said the transfer of Lebanese prisoners to Israel

appears to be inconsistent with Geneva Convention regulations governing war prisoners.

29. It was January when President Reagan decided to nominate Rep. Sam Hall for the

federal bench.

30. Billy Hugh Fullerton, 30, of Corsicana was killed when he lost control of the car,

which ran off the highway and hit a tree.

31. Williams, who worked as a draftsman for 10 years before losing his sight, had sold

one piece of sculpture.

32. A novice cave explorer who slipped and became wedged in a narrow crevice died

Monday despite the efforts of rescue workers who spent 34 hours an arm's length away.

Your name _____

Date _____

33. The body of the drowning victim was recovered at about 4 p.m.

34. The professors said their main desire was for improved financial support and less

onerous workloads.

35. If the period of the truce were used by the enemy to build up bases, the Allied

advantage would largely disappear.

36. Eleven plans for removing troops gradually have been worked out through the years

by the United Nations.

37. The City Council was forced to call for a bond election, or, alternately, raise taxes.

38. There is nothing that can devastate a household budget faster than illness.

39. Chancellor Charles Le Maister, the report said, is a man who is competent both in

medicine as well as the field of philosophy.

40. The sponsors of two competing no-fault auto accident insurance bills have amended

their respective measures to meet criticism levied against them.

41. The two planes collided over the Grand Canyon at an altitude of 8,000 feet.

42. The senator rose to the defense of the president's nomination for the Circuit Court, but

Your name _____

... **clutter,** continued

Date _____

later he took the floor and readily admitted that he had not had enough time to study the

nominee's record.

43. Doctors gave Vince Balsinger of Santa Ana, Calif., a new heart in a transplant

operation a week ago.

44. The commission dropped the idea of ordering more uniforms for summer baseball.

45. The spring storm left the crops under a blanket of snow 5 inches deep.

46. The fact that Johnson did not act sooner cost him the support of his remaining backers.

47. The car spun, skidded 25 feet and came to a stop before entering the intersection.

48. The House promised to take all necessary measures to see that tax breaks would go to

the middle class.

49. The dean said all students who are interested in participating in the tryouts were urged

to be there at 9 a.m. Monday morning.

50. Three young girls were bruised and slightly injured Wednesday when a railroad

locomotive scraped the rear end of an automobile in which they were riding as passengers.

Libel and ethics

Libel, ethics — Exercise 1

In this section you have an advantage over real life: You get a warning that the material contains libel or bad taste or both. Normally, news stories don't come with warnings. However, they do contain signs, and a little practice will help you pick up some of those signs. See what you can pick up in the following sentences. Edit for libel, taste, fairness, grammar, spelling and about anything else you can think of. The paragraphs are unrelated to each other. You have two extra options: 1. You may kill any sentence you cannot salvage. 2. You may leave untouched any sentence you consider safe and proper to run unchanged.

1. A Brightsville man, Sean Gutenberg, was arrested 20 minutes after robbing the store.

2. The district attorney said he would file murder charges against the suspect, Earl

Koonce, as soon as he had talked with one more witness.

3. Police caught up with Koonce on Burnet Road, headed out of town. He was arrested

without resistance.

4. Leo Fields, who was charged with murder, lives at 397-A Deep Eddy Apartments.

Ironically, another murderer lived in that same apartment only two years ago.

5. Police scoured the grounds and found the robber behind some garbage in an alley.

6. Jones fled the scene after running the girl down. He said after his arrest for hit-and -

un driving that he did not feel his truck hit the girl.

7. Builder Earl O'Keefe, who has had trouble getting financing for his Hidden Bayou

Apartments, will probably have to file for bankruptcy under Chapter 11, one of his

creditors said Tuesday. O'Keefe had no comment

... **exercise 1,** continued

8. The police chief has generally been considered an incompetent oaf by his men and by

the city administration.

9. Cougarade is an atrocious drink. It claims to have a million vitamins—and it has a

drop of bitter taste for every one of them.

10. Congressman Flake called candidate Yarber "an infamous baboon who should forget

his plans for foisting himself upon the unsuspecting public."

11. Priscilla Martin opened her one-woman show at the Art Museum yesterday. Old Priss

should stick to finger painting and forget about an art career. She might try painting barns.

12. N.G. Davies, an assistant city attorney, was taken to Memorial Hospital yesterday

after an attempt to cut his wrists. His landlady foiled the suicide attempt.

13. E.R. Ralfernst 70, of 204 Long Street, died in a car wreck yesterday.

14. Ralph Ernst, 1207 Elm Terrace, died of leprosy yesterday.

15. Ernst Ralph, 7021 Mel Drive, died of AIDS yesterday.

16. The two dancing sisters looked more like salami than Salome. They inflicted

themselves on a suffering audience for five minutes—it seemed like two hours—at the

halftime of the basketball game.

Libel, ethics — Exercise 2

Examine the following sentences for taste and make corrections as appropriate. Correct all other errors, too.

1. Sheriff's deputies found the body of a 12-year-old girl in a corn patch Monday. Because of the advanced state of decomposition of the body, the identification was not immediately determined. The medical examiner said that the blackened state of the flesh and the way it was peeling from the bones indicated that the death occurred two weeks ago.

2. Highway patrolmen who investigated the accident described it as the worst they had seen. They said body parts and even some body organs were strewn over the highway and that an arm was found 300 feet from the crash site.

3. When the mayor becomes excited, he has trouble with a speech impediment that has afflicted him since he was a child. During a heated argument friday with Councilman Bob James, the mayor, who appeared to be losing the battle, told James: "Just si-si-sit down shu-shu-shu-shut up."

4. For years a citizen group has been trying to get City Hall to take action against the pigeons, which roost in the oak trees and heavily decorate the cars that are parked underneath. "We've had about all the pigeon do-do we can take," said the group's leader.

... **exercise 2,** continued

5. Elred brought suit against the cereal company, seeking $5 million for mental anguish after he found a huge cockroach at the bottom of his cereal bowl.

6. Complaints about the food in the Jester Center cafeteria have almost become a tradition. Cafeteria wags like to tell about the person who sat down with a tray of food, looked at it in despair, and said: "I hope this tastes better to me than it did to the person who puked it onto this tray."

7. Records show that since Mel Tillis started promoting sales for a hamburger chain, business has increased 25 percent nationwide. Tillis, who doesn't stutter when he sings but does otherwise, said, "That's gr-gr-gre-great."

8. Despite his unpopularity, the headmaster, often called "Gus the Gimp" because of a limp that remains from a 1985 car accident, has turned the Union High into one of the state's most respected prep schools.

9. The movie makes the mistake of resurrecting a hoary tune with paraphrased lyrics, but it does not work as parody as the director intended. The main verse goes like this: "I don't want your greenback dollar, I don't want your golden watch and chain; all I want is your .45 pistol to blow out your no-good brains."

10. A farm laborer lost an ear in a farm accident near Jonesboro Tuesday and is reported in stable condition at Memorial Hospital. The worker, Jose Maldonado, was operating a hay baler when he was thrown off the machine after it hit a bump. Maldonado became entangled in the machine. The accident apparently has not affected Maldonado's sense of humor, nurses in his ward say. They say he invariably smiles when he is greeted by nurses, who usually kid him by saying, "Jose, can you hear?"

11. A 2-year old boy was killed this morning when he fell from his parents' camper on the highway and was run over by a truck.

The child, Earl Dean Koonce, son of Mr. and Mrs. Earl Dean Koonce, 1177 Kenedy Lane, Brightsville, died instantly. The truck's left front tire smashed the child's skull and other tires flattened the tiny body, said a witness, Earl Creech. "It was horrible, horrible," said Creech, who was splattered with blood though he was standing more than 15 feet from the highway when the tires squashed the baby.

Investigating officers theorized that the child awoke from a nap and somehow opened the back door. No charges were filed against the parents despite their failure to secure the door. "They feel pretty bad about this," said Sheriff's Deputy Bill Plumley.

Libel, ethics — fairness exercise

In addition to worrying about libel, you need to consider fairness. Sometimes you can legally say things you don't really need to say. Some of the sentences below could get you sued, and some could just get you criticized. Reconstruct these sentences so that whatever blame they place will be based only on known facts. Material in parentheses adds facts for you to use in editing, if you wish.

1. Police said the driver was speeding. (Speed: 34 mph; limit: 30.)

2. Police said the driver was intoxicated. (He did .12 on Breathalyzer, and .10 is the legal line.)

3. The red LeBaron hit the blue Park Avenue at the intersection.

4. Smith and Jones argued. Then Smith stabbed Jones. (A witness says this.)

5. As the pickup pulled alongside the station wagon, the driver of the pickup fired three shots into the right front door of the station wagon.

6. The president of the airline was responsible for the accident because he gave the order to use a lower grade of fuel.

7. Smith killed the policeman with three shots from a .22-caliber revolver.

8. The boy was arrested for taking a box of candy from the drug store. (He was charged with a misdemeanor.)

9. Smith was indicted for murder.

... fairness, continued

10. The pickup ran a stop a sign and hit the station wagon in the middle of the intersection.

(The pickup's driver was charged with running a stop sign.)

11. George Malefactor fled the store with $2,000 from the cash register. He was caught at

a roadblock 20 minutes later. The money from the store was found in a paper bag on the

back seat of his car. Malefactor was arrested for robbery. (The charge was filed.)

12. Tom Lean dined at the Creek cafe on raw oysters, which made him ill and caused him

to be hospitalized for food poisoning.

13. The maid apparently killed four neighborhood dogs by placing poisoned meat in the

front yard of her employer's house. The dogs were found dead the week of March 16.

Investigators said they found 10 pounds of aresenic-laced meat in the maid's car, which

was searched after a warrant was issued. The maid has not been charged.

14. A 70-year-old woman who lost a fight to keep a sewer line off her land was arrested

today for shoting at a surveying crew and two sheriff's deputies. (She was charged.)

15. A search of the car produced nearly an ounce of marijuana. The driver was arrested

for possession of a controlled substance and was taken to jail.

. . . fairness, continued

16. Tragedy has been no stranger to the family. A second son, age 20, is severely

retarded and is kept in diapers in a separate room.

17. The cyanide poisoner's parents, Mr. and Mrs. Martin Elred, recently moved to

Brightsville. They live at 1121 Snahttgnoze Blvd, and their phone number is 471-1998.

18. The father of the defected CIA agent, Erath Bell Travis, said his son had called from

Moscow and asked the Travises to come visit him. Travis, who works for a defense

contractor, said he would not go until after his retirement in five years. He said he was

afraid of trouble at the plant because of its defense ties and the secrets his son had taken to

the U.S.S.R..

19. Chanel 11 anchorwoman Megan Muffeay was raped Thursday by a masked intruder in

her posh West Brightsville condo. Muffeay, 36, said the attack occurred as she returned

home at midnight, after completing her day's work at KTTV-TV. She suffered a cracked

jaw and a black eye.

Libel, ethics — robbery exercise

Edit this story as your instructor suggests.

Two men were today placed under arest and charged with the robbery or attempted robbery of three places and the shooting of a motel clerk.

Raymond Martin was shot about 1:20 a.m. today as two men attempted to holdup the Holliday Inn Skouth, 20 North IH 35. LThe Cross Country Inn at U.S. 290 and IH 35 was robbed at 11:59 p.m. yesterday, police stated.

Homicide Det. Roger Rountree said this morning that the two roberies and attempted robbery were linked together.

Donnel Gordon, 22, of 2 000 East. 12th Street, and Santone Smith, 30, of 2004 E. 12th Street, were held in City jail without bond after being ch arged with assault to committ murder in conection with the shooting early today of Martin at the Holiday Inn's attempted stickup. Martin was listed critical condition at Memorial's Intensive care Unit late this morning with a gunshot would inthe left chest , according to a hospital spokesman wh gave out information to the working press.

The police said Marten was shot with a 22 calibre pistol about 1 a.m. when an armed

... **robbery,** continued

robbery attempt perpertrated by two masked men at the Holliday Inn South went awry.

Miss Ann Mabry of 1801 W. 35th St., night auditor at the Holiday Inn South said she

was behind the desk in the Inn's office when two Negro men came in the front door.

One of the men pulled a gun and pointed it directly at her, and then he jumped onto the

counter, Miss Mabry said. Night operator Phillip Lyrer, 55, of 165 E. Wensley, came to

the counter and told the man to leave, Miss Mabry sayed.

The armed gunman, apparently starteled, fell over backwards off the inn's counter,

investigating officers said Miss Marby said.

At thatt moment, Miss Mabry said she heard a gunshot and the man who had leapt onto

the counter and later fallen ran out the front door of the inn.

licesaid the gunshot was fired byu the man who had been with the gunman who talked

toMabry. The auditor said she did not see the other man leave.

Martin was found in a pool of blood on third floor of the 13-story inn, police said.

Investigators theorized Martin had been trying to get to the third floor apartment of

Inkeepper Don Newwel. The bell captain was apparently shot in the back as he approached

. . . robbery, continued

the stairs in the inn's lobby, and was able to make it up three flights of stairs to the thid

floor before he collapsed, according to the police officers who investigated the attempted

robbery.

Police said the description given by employees at the Holiday Inn Soth matched

perfectly the information given by the night cleark at the Corss Country Inn.

Brent Couldin, 21, of 2380 Del Curton, on duty at the time of the hold-up of the North

side motel, said a man came into the office about 11:30 p.m. yesterday and asked about

renting a room. Bouldin said when he told the man the price the man, a Negro said, "Too

high," and left.

About 20 minutes later the man returned accompanied by another man. The duet robbed

the motel, taking Boulden's wallet and stealing all the money out of the cash register.

Smith was arrested with Gordon in the 1800 block of Corona Circle about 10 a.m. this

morning. Police said a tipster tipped them off after hearing smith and Gordon talking in a

restaurant.

Smith was also charged before Muniiciple Judge Roland Sloan in the 3 p.m. yesterday

Your name _____

Date _____

... robbery, continued

robbery of the Goodwill Industries Store. The Goodwill heist netted an undisclosed amount

of Money. An armed gunman, wearing a stocking mask over his face, held up cashier

Mrs. Daily Holt after racing into the store. Only two clerks were on duty.

A word on math

Your name_____

Date_____

Figures give us all trouble. People make math mistakes in all kinds of publications—quarterly magazines, monthlies, weeklies, dailies. Every time you see a numeral, you see a chance for a mistake. You must develop the habit of checking all figures.

But that does not mean a perfect copy editor will catch every mistake. Certainly it does not mean a perfect copy editor can **correct** every mistake; you must often go back to the reporter for information. For instance, you have no way to tell whether a reporter left off a name or miscounted if the reporter says 49 students won prizes . . . and lists 48.

If that's not enough, you also have to check logic. In the following exercise, you must decide what error of logic has been made, what figure has been left out and what is needed to make these other figures meaningful. You do not need to edit the stories.

1. Salaries of the top three executives went up a total of 48 percent—19 percent for Williams, 16 percent for Abrams and 13 percent for Mach.

2. Last year, sharks attacked nearly 12 times as many male swimmers as females off U.S. beaches. Professor Elred believes one of the sexes' body chemistry gives off a slightly different odor that causes sharks to either avoid or attack persons of that sex.

3. Dr. Fower Sepps reported that 65 percent to 68 percent of his patients who take birth control pills suffer discomfort from contact lenses.

4. Fifteen nations have improved their infant mortality rates more than the United States since 1950, clearly indicating a decline in health care in this country.

5. Among 95 percent of the couples seeking divorce, one or both partners do not attend church regularly, the vicar said in concluding that churchgoers stay married.

6. Jones showed data indicating that his new engine runs 40 percent cooler.

7. Starlife bread contains only three-fourths as many calories per slice as other breads.

8. The provost noted that one third of the women who entered the university's first class to allow females had married faculty members.

9. The average age at which Brightsville boys start shaving is 16.537 years.

10. Executives of the company own an average of 600 shares of Tracor stock.

Your name _____

Date _____

Math — Editing exercise

Edit this story as your instructor suggests.

The price of oil in international markets showd signs of stabalizing today, though they were still sharply lower after a week's fall caused by a world suprplus of supplies. At the close of trading on the Mercantile Exchange yesterday, contracts for delivery of West Texas Intermediate, the top U.S. crude grade, stood at $19.50 a barrel, down 32 cents from the previous day's $19.92. A barrel is the equivalent of 42 gallons, making the $19.50 price break down to 46.43 cents per gallon of unrefined oil. Elsewhere, North Sea oil for delivery in April sold for $18.65 a barel, up 45 cents from the previous day's $18.30. That $18.65 tag was down more than a dollar from the previous week. The price of heating oil was down again, but gasolene prices rose slightly. Although the market had shown signs of settling down recently, prices were still 26 percent less than they were six months ago, when a a barrel of West TExas Internmediate sold for $25.15 and 30 percent less than they were nine months ago when a barrel cost $31.70. Most of the decline from that $31.70 tag to the $25.15 occurred in 10 days, rather than as a steady slide.

. . . **editing exercise,** continued

The Organization of Petroleum Exporting Countries announced late in 1985 that it was

giving up attempts to support prices by controling production. The 12 cartel members said

they would pursue their "fair market share" instead. That meant an increase in production.

Although the world was already awash in oil, supplies swelled, pushing prices downward

amid O.P.E.C. warnings of a price war. The situation stabilized in the summer of 1986

when OPEC members reached another agreement. OPEC members are Algeria, Gabon,

Indonesia, Iran, Iraq, Kuwait, Libya, Nigeria, Quatar, Saudi Arabia, United Arab

Emirates, Venezuela and Ecaudor.

Your name _____

Date _____

Editing—filling holes

As sort of a warmup for a heavy-duty section on editing, we are going to look at some stories with holes. Your job here is to decide what questions were not answered in these stories. What else would readers need to make the story more undertstandable? You do not need to edit these stories.

1. A Houston halfway house counselor was charged today with hindering arrest after he allegedly warned a murder suspect living in the house that the police wanted him.

The suspect, Louis Wright Jr., 21, is charged with capital murder in the June 1 shooting deaths of Lawrence Watkins, 22, and his wife, Judith Ann, 20.

Police say the counselor, John Bradly Carroll, 25, of 4514 Holt, told Wright Tuesday that he was wanted and that Wright's father and lawyer knew where he was.

Wright's father, Louis Sr., told police he informed Carroll of the murder charge, said he wanted to see his son, and cautioned the councelor twice not to alert his son.

2. A Houston teen-ager drowned in Lake Houston near Dessau Park yesterday while swimming to a concession stand.

The youth, Leroy Dale Jones of 20206 Havdock, drowned at 2:30 p.m. His body was recovered at 3:45 p.m. by park police.

Jones, his twin brother, Jerry, and another man were swimming across a boat channel to reach a concession stand when Jones disappeared.

3. When Tom Backus, general manager of IBM, arrived at Symphony Square to complete IBM's three-part donation the the cultural project, he found the place going to the dogs.

The century-old structure, recently moved to the square from 1125 Red River, had become the home of four pups discovered beneath the old New Orleans Club.

Renovation of the rock and rubble edifice will produce the new Orleans Club Mercantile.

The complex, aided federally by Urban Renewal and Civically by Symphony Square benefactors, includes three additional historic buildings. They will house the Brightsville Symphony's general business offices, an arts and craft shop, and a music and youth center.

Completing the square is a 500-seat grass ampitheater and a hike-and-bike trail along the banks of Waller Creek. The entire project is aimed at generating funds to support the symphony.

In addition the the pup named Willie Nelson, which Backus acquired, the three remaining pups—Mozart, Bach and Beethoven—chose to stay sheltered beneath the historic building.

4. The deadline for getting funds needed to preserve the Wild Basin of Bee Creek, outside Brightsville's city limits, as a public nature park has been extended from Saturday to an indefinite date, the Committee for Wild Basin Wilderness Park announced today.

...holes, continued

The Advisory Committee for Fund Raising met at the Governor's Mansion to discuss possible projects and the acquisition of land.

The group filed an application for $475,000 in matching federal funds to buy the 15-acre Masel tract and two more tracts in the area, The deadline for purchase of the Masel Tract was a week from Sunday. A fourth tract is being held for the group by a private individual until the funds can be raised.

5. One Brightsville youth was missing and presumed drowned and two others were left injured yesterday after a motorboat ran over them on Lake Bunge as they tried to right their overturned canoe.

Donald Murphy, 38, operator of the boat, was being held in the City Jail under $15,000 bail.

Missing in the northeast Brightsville lake is Jack Taylor, 13, son of Mr. and Mrs. Layne Taylor, 5603 Lakewood Terrace.

Clarence Mix, 10, son of Mr. and Mrs. Ross Mix of 6408 Chester, was treated at Memorial Hospital for cuts on his right leg. Danny Port, 11, son of Mr. and Mrs. Allen Port, suffered a minor cut on his right leg but did not require hospital treatment.

Police officials said a charge of involuntary manslaughter will be taken to the Center County Grand Jury if young Taylor is dead.

Police and survivors of the incident gave the following account: The youths, on a canoe outing sponsored by the Running R Day Camp, had just righted their capsized canoe when one lost a paddle. As they treaded water to retrieve the paddle, a boat that had been nearby suddenly started up and passed over the three boys.

Only Mix and Port, who were wearing life jackets, surfaced and swam back to the overturned canoe.

Police took Murphy, who was driving the boat, and a passenger, Hyman Calloway, 35, of Guymon, Okla., to headquarters for questioning.

Later, Murphy was taken before Municipal Judge Alberto Garcia and charged with the second degree felony. Calloway was released after paying a fine for public intoxication.

6. A boating accident on Lake Bunge, which left 14-year-old Jack Taylor dead, was the first tragedy the Running R Day Camp has ever had, but it was not a total surprise for city park rangers.

Mrs. Norris Davoux, camp director, said the camp usually has 100-115 youths a day and has 24 licensed adults on the staff to supervise them.

Tom Alben said Tuesday that his city park rangers "had anticipated" a problem on Lake Bunge for the last two or three months because of a general increase in activity on the popular boating-swimming spot.

Alben said his department had requested two new rangers and a boat, all specifically intended for work at Bunge, but had not received them yet.

Mrs. Davoux said Taylor, who apparently drowned after being hit by a boat, was one of the camp's least likely candidates for a water accident. She said she spoke to the youth's mother only the day before the accident and remarked about what a good swimmer he was. Taylor was a junior counselor. As such, he could supervise other youths in their water activities.

Your name _____

Date _____

Editing — Fire exercise

Edit this as your instructor directs. If it sounds familiar, that's because some of it comes from your textbook. Edit it here before turning to the book for advice.

Holton, Kans. (GLP)—A smouldering divan caught fire early this morning,

destroying a turn of the century hotel and killing five elderly residents.

State Fire Marshal Floyd Dibbern said investigators blame carless smoking for the fire at

City Hotel.

Dibbern said the fire began early today in a divan in Albert Jardine's room. He said

Jardine, 54, left the door to his room adjar when he went to tell the manager that somke

was coming from the divan.

When he left the door open, it let air in," Bibbern said. "A woman reported it sounded

like a small explosion. What she heard was a back draft. Wehen oxygen got to it, it really

took off."

Witnesses at the scene said Jardine went back into the building to save his cat. Dibbern

said, because of the location of Jardin's body, he thinks Jardine actually returned to

awaken other residents.

"It went up just like that, Holton fire chief warren Baum said. "When we got to the

. . . fire, continued

scene, the rear of the hotel was totally involved. The fire was poking through the roof."

Officials identified the dead folks as Jardine, Mike HOdges, 75, Marguerite Pauline

Hayes, 83, Ev Williams, 63, and Adolph Posten, 70.

Baum said 24 persons were registerd in the two-story brick structure. Many of them

walked out of their first floor rooms but several residents on the second floor jumped to

safety or slid down ropes ancored inside their rooms.

"There was no fire escape on the building," Dibbern said, "what they had were dead-

end corridors."

The fire marshall said his office has no record indicating City Hotel was ever inspected

by the state.

"We've already been inspecting these hotels wand wer'e finding them like this all over

the state, Dibbern said.

"They're either going to have to bring them up to the code—put fire excapes on them

and have alarms on them—or their not going to operate."

Dibbern said a fire in Auugust that killed five young men in a Baker University frat

house has spurred his department's investigations of such multistoried residents.

. . . fire, continued

Two residents of City Hotel were injured when they jumped from second stroy

windows. Another escaped by means of an old-fashioned fire escape made of chains.

Chester Frear, 23, an amublance attendent who suffered back injuries, sprains and

contusions when he slipped in a muddy spot, also was hospitalized.

Among the residents who walked out of their first floor rooms was Alf Landon, who

ran for president against Franklin Roosevelt in 1936. Landon,l now 90, has lived in the

hotel, which sits on his birth site, for 11 years now. He owns the hotel, witnesses at the

fire scene told reporters.

The hotel doesnot have a no-smoking section. Residents are or were allowed to smoke

anywhere in the building. "I knew one of those old coots would set the place on far one of

these days," said witness Earl Durier, who saw the fire at 2 a.m. or 2:l5, just after the bars

closed. Durier lives across the street at Crost ARms, another residence hotel. He has been

there 14 years and said he has been expecting a fire ever since he arrived.

Editing — Census exercise

Edit this story as your instructor suggests. Watch for style problems.

WASHINGTON (GLP)—Rapidly growing Phoenix, Arizona, has replaced Boston as the largest capital city in the United States of America.

New Census Bureau figures show Phoenix with a population of 878,266, the largest of any capital city in the nation. Boston was listed fourth with 590,354 residents.

But Boston had enjoyed first place for many decades and still is often thought to be the largest capital because it serves as the business, political and cultural center of New England.

New York City is still the nation's largest City.

Until the 1980 census, Boston led the list of the most populated state capitals.

Boston had 748,060 residents in 1920, 801,444 in 1950, 697,197 in 1960 and 641,071 in 1970, compared with Phoenix's 29,053 in 1920, 106,818 in 1950, 439,170 in 1960 and 584,303 in 1970. The Boston area has gained population, but much of it has been in suburbs. The Boston metro area is considerably more populous than Phoenxi. Phoenix has a large outlying area within its city limits.

... **census,** continued

Boston placed fourth in the latest list of most populous capital cities, behind Phoenix,

Honolulu, and Indianapolis, in that order.

The least-populated capital city in the latest tally was Montpelier, Vermont, with a

population of 8,280. In 1920 and 1950, the least-populated capital was Carson City, Nev.

Meg Greenbloss, a statistician with the Massachusetts Data Center, said Boston lost

residents to suburban areas in Massachusetts in the 1970s and 1980s. Shee said the state's

population has shifted from the Boston area in the northeastern part of the state to the Cape

Cod area in the southeast.

The latest census figures show the exodus from Boston has slowed and that some

people are moving back into the downtown area, Greenbloss added.

She said many still consider Boston the largest capital city because it is centered around

a strong downtown area, unlike in the West.

"The comparison of a city in Arizona to Massachusetts is really difficult—at least

psychologically, they are so different," Murray said.

A Census Bureau statistician, pointed out that Eastern and Midwestern cities have been

losing population and businesses to the South and Southwest for two decades.

Much of Arizonas gain is due more to "push factors," such as bad weather or lack of

... **census,** continued

jobs in Ohio, than to the attraction that Phoenix might present, Hansen said.

She said the closings of "smokestack" industries in the Midwest and of the shoes and

textile industries in New England fueled the migration to the South and Southwest.

Hansen also said there is less difference today among the cultural amenities and the

caliber of educational institutions from city to city.

Migration also is attributed to the appealing climate in the Southwest, jobs in such

growth industries as "high technology" and the relatively low cost of living outside the East

and Midwest.

Max Murray, a researcher for the Arizona Department of Economic Security, said

Phoenix's population doubled from 1920 to 1930. It quadrupled between 1950 and 1960.

Phoenix passed Tucson as Arizona';s largest city between 1910 and 1920, taking the

lead officially after the 1920 census.

The suburban areas of Mesa, Glendale, Scottsdale and Tempe are growing at even faster

rates.,

Mesa grew 141 percent from 1970 to 1980; Glendale 168 percent; Chandler, 115

percent; Scottsdale, 30.7 percent and Temple, 68 percent.

Editing — Gadhafi exercise

Edit this story to the length your instructor suggests. Correct all errors, including those of grammar, spelling and style

WASHINGTON—The president has reportedly authorized a secret CIA operation to undermine the government of Libya's Col. Moammar Gadhafi. The move signals a resumption of activity in the Mideast, where the U.S.A. lost a great amount of presitige in the arms-for-hostages fiasco with Iran.

Usually reliable goverment sources say the plan involves supplying aid to North African and Middle East nations that oppose Gadhafi. It has run into resistance from the Congressional committees that oversee the CIA, which would operate the clandestine operation. The chairman and vice chairman of the Senate Intelligence Committee recently outlined their opposition to the covert operation in a letter to the President.

Even so, a slima narrow majority on that panel and the House Intelligence Committee supports the covert action, administration sources said. Secy. of State George Shultz appeared before the House committee as recently as last week to support the plan.

Sources said the operation would try to disrupt and frustrate Gadhafi 's subversive and terrorist plans in the area and in the rest of the world.

... **Gadhafi,** continued

Secondly, they said, it might make him attmpt some adventure or terrerist exploit that would give his opponents in the Libyan military a chance to seize power, or Gadhafi might do something to give a country like Algeria or Egypt, justification for stepping in.

The White House has had largely ineffective economic sanctions in pace for 5 1/2 years. Now it has decided that Gadhafi is such an international menace that secret steps to topple him should be undertaken, officials said.

Shultz and the CIA director have reportedly said the new covert plan is designed to stop terrorism, not to support the assasination of Gadhafi , sources said.

A longstanding Executive Order forbids the CIA or any government agency from involvement in assasinations.

This is the issue that most concerns the chairman and vice chairman of the Senate Select Intelligence Committee, David Durenberger, Rep., Minn., and Patrick Leahy (D-Vt.), respectively, who conveyed their opposition to the plan against Gadhafi in a letter to the White House, in which they asked how the plan would avoid the prohibition against assasination attempts or plans.

... **Gadhafi,** continued

The White House responded, sources said, by insisting that there is no plan to assasinate Gadhafi.

Administration sources admit that the president, secretary of state and CIA head would like to see Gadhafi toppled and believe that a support operation through a third country is the type of anti-terrorist operation that can safely and legally be undertaken.

Gadhafi reportedly supports about 30 radical groups around the world, most of them anti-American or opposed to US interests.

A 1984, report from US intelligence agencies said, ":No course of action short of stimulating Gadhafi 's fall will bring any significant and enduring change in Libyan policies."

Any weaknesses in Libya could only be exploited, the assessment said, "through a broad program in cooperation with key countries, combining political, economic and paramilitary action."

"The exile groups, if supported to a substantial degree, could soon begin an intermitten campaign of sabotage and violence which could prompt further challenges to Gadhafi's authority," it added.

... **Gadhafi,** continued

Egypt, Iraq, Morocco, Saudi Arabia, Sudan and Tunisia have all supported Libyan

exiles who stand in opposition to the desert-loving Gadhafi.

The State Department intelligence branch has different ideas about the vulnerability

assessment. One official said it "rests too heavily on fragmentary, unsubstantiated

reporting and fails to give sufficient weight to Gadhaffi 's enduring popularity."

Gadhafi has been nettlesome to the administration since 1981, the first year of the

Reagan presidency. Gadhafi allegedly dispatched "hit teams" to assassinate the president

or other top U.S. officials at that time.

The president has authority to begin covert operations which he deems necessary for the

national security. However, federal laws require him to notifie the congressional

overseeing committees promptly. Congress cannot order the president to stop an

operation, but it can cut off funds, as was done in Nicaragua.

An alternative to an attempt to overthrow Gadhafi might be some support to Egypt or

Algeria, although both of those nations have had serious reservations about cooperating in

past anti-Gadhafi proposals.

... **Gadhafi,** continued

CIA Dputy Director John McMahon is said to have blocked a move on Gadhafi last year on grounds that the exiles planning it were "babes in the woods" and too weak to have even half a chance at success.

The CIA director supported that no-go decision, inside sources reported, because no U.S. ally would support an uprising. Intelligence sources say Gadhafi picked up some respectability in Europe laset year, expanding intelligence ties with Greece and enhancing military relations with Italy and Turkey.

One new intelligence report says Gadhafi is stirring up subversion in Chad, Sudan and Tunisia; backing the "radical states" of Iran, Syria, Ethiopia and Nicaragua; continuing support to groups in the Philippines, New Caledonia, Pakistan and Zaire; an supporting insurgents or terrorist groups in Guatemala, El Salvador, Chile, Colombia, the Dominican Republic, Lebanon and Iraq.

The same intelligence estimate said there were 50,000 Soviet and East European technicians or advisers in Libya.

Such special intelligence estimates come through the CIA (Central Intelligence Agency), with input from the other U.S. intelligence agencies.

. . . **Gadhafi,** continued

In early 1986, Libya military officiers launched two unsuccessful assasination attempts

against Gadhafi. He executed as many as 75 officers accused of participating in them.

Reports that Gadhafi is planning actions against U.S. installations or citizens come in

regularly. Many are considered from reliable sources.

One report said Gadhafi had formed two special commando and terrorist units.

Editing — Sewer exercise

Edit this story as your instructor suggests.

Brightsville's plans to extend sewer service to four suburbs may be scaled back unless

$700,000 more can be found to pay for the proposed system, council members heard last

night.

The groundbreaking date has been pushed back at least six months, said Bobby

McClain, of McClain Engineeering. It was originally scheduled for the first of next month.

The city council also set a special meeting for 6 p.m. next Tuesday to hear the results of

the annual audit.

Otto Knotto, the sewer project engineer for the city, told the council that scaling back

would not omit current residents from services, but would allow for less growth than

originally planned for the first phase.

The project already is designed to be expandable, he said.

The increased cost of the $9 million project comes from differences between the original

concept and technical aspects found to be necessary during the design stage.

Knotto said flood protection proved to be more expensive than originally thought, and

. . . sewer, continued

larger pipes will have to be run to carry sewage frm Big Bear resort to the plant facility.

Purchase of the land and easements also cost more than originally thought, he said.

In other business, the council was told that groundbreaking for the Big Sur resort is

still anticipated next month. The city has applied for $72,000 in federal funds for the

city's job training program.

Outgoing city councilman Alf Flowers reported that plans for a wider bridge over

Coldwater River are moving, and the state and hopes to complete construction late next

year.

Bridge builder Charles Miller said he is grateful to Flowers for efforts to hasten

improvements on Guadalupe, a state highway that bisects six cities and communities,

including El Mirage.

"We're not doing this to take credit, we've been defeated," Flowers said. He praised

the winners of Tuesday's primary for a well-run campaign.

"I wish we had put together a campaign like that, but we were too busy with city

projects," Flowers said. "If you continue progress for the city, that's all that matters. We

hope you take the ball and go through the doors we worked so hard to open."

. . . sewer, continued

Flowesrs and running mates councilmen Dan Saunders and Manny Figueres lost their

seats to Betty Himmelblau, Marylu Isaacs and Don Winslow, each of whom won without

a runoff by pulling more than 50 percent of the vote in the primary election. Councilman

John Deutch retained his seat in the primary vote.

Flowers offered his help to the new council members, who will take their seats in May.

Winslow, who headed the slate that won the primary, thanked Flowers. "You three

have a lot of experience and we would be fools not ask you for help."

The four suburbs that had asked for sewer service, which they would pay for with

direct rate increases, are Jonnem, Quinn, Griff Inn and Senger. The city also has a legal

committment to provide sewer service to Big Bear resort, starting the first of next month.

Editing — Teachers exercise

Delete at least 10 but no more than 15 lines from this story. Be sure to retain its general flavor. Make all necessary corrections.

New teachers entering the educational systems this year will face a gamut of

requirments before receiving full certification in two years.

According to the new guidelines of the State Department of Public Instruction published

last month and outlined in the Monday night meting of the Brightsville City School board,

teachers have stricter requirements to prove themselves able before being granted state

accreditation.

As Moore explained, the Initial Teacher Certification Program is a newly-devised plan

focused on "any person coming out of a teacher training program (who) will receive an

initial certificate good for only two years."

During the two-year period, the teacher will receive guidance from the principal and

experienced teachers will also be working with them and evaluating their progress. At the

end of the two-year period a decision wil be made as to whether the teacher will be granted

or denied certification.

. . . teachers, continued

The initial certification will not only affect incoming college grads seeking teaching jobs but also any out-of-statae transfer teachers irregardless of the amount of their experience they may have elsewhere.

Local teacher association President Margaret Burchette asked if the program would affect an already certified teacher who changed to another career field for a few years and then came beck to the teaching profession.

"I don't think it will," Moore said, saying that once the teacher has been certified and maintained those certification standards that they would not be required to meet the two-year stint.

Assistant Superintendent Mary Sharpe Owens said the local systemwill affiliate itself with a nearby university, such as Eastern State, in order to be eligible to receive candidates from the teacher education program

"We will need to affiliate with Eastern State or some other, similar, university before we are able to get candidates from the program, Owens said.

According to the guidelines, if the students fail to meet the qualificatons to graduate

... **teachers,** continued

from the teacher education program, they will be denied the initial certificate. Teachers may

opt to recycle through the courses or go into another career field. Once they are on the job,

if teachers fail to meet the standards required by the local education agency after two years

in the classroom, continuing certification will be denied. They may either exit the program

or return to college to take additional education courses. In discussing the new

certification, Mrs. Owens pointed out there had bben ominous warnings by some state

officials of educational administrators about another teacher shortage by the end ofthe

decade

    As a result, a proposal will be reviewed by the state leegislature next summer regarding

a "Lateral Entry Plan." The plan may grant teacher certification to people with experienced

technical bacckgrounds or who have had on=the-the-job training in other areas for enought

time to make them knowledgeable in the area.

    Board member Carey Washburn pointefd out this type of program is in effect already in

some other states and appears to be working well.

Editing — Lawyer exercise

Edit this story as your instructor suggests.

A defense lawyer who intentionally lost a case to protest his heavy caseload in

Brightsville Municipal Court hjas been ordered to face a contempt hearing.

Attorney Herb Garamond expressed "shock" at the ruling of Central County Superior

Court Judge Rudy Heinz.

"Gee whiz! I did everything I could," Garamond said. "I work hard for my clients,

and I ask for time to prepare, that's all."

Heinz ruled that Garamond, a court appointed attorney, failed to prepare for the drunken

driving trial involving Lydia Legleu, 19, of Brightsville.

Heinz wrote in a memo to the State Bar that Garamond refused to help pick the jury, that

he did not cross-examine witnesses, that he made no opening statement or closing

argument, and that he otherwise failed to carry out his obligation to his clients.

Garamond "adopted the foregoing course of behavior in order to dramatize his work

load problems" in Municipal Court, Heinz wrote.

Your name _____

Date_____

. . . **lawyer,** continued

A jury convicted Legleu of drunken-driving.

Heinz overturned the conviction and ruled that Legleu must receive a new trial in
Municpal Court. Heinz ruled that results of Garamond's contempt hearing must be sent to
the State Bar Association.

And he ordered a Municipal Court judge to consider forcing Garamond to return any
money he received while defending Legleu.

No date has been set for the contempt hearing.

Garamond told *The Brightsville Gazette* in May that his "head might be on the chopping
block with the State Bar" because of his decision not to defend Legleu, but he added that
the ploy was the only way he could offer his client any hope of winning.

He said his large caseload made it impossible for him to interview witnesses for the case
and that he tried without success to postpone the trial. When the trial began, he decided to
sit back and do nothing while a prosecutor presented the state's case and a jury heard the
evidence and then convicted Legleu, he said.

Garamond then appealed the conviction to Superior Court on grounds that his heavy
workload worked a burden on him and his client, in this case Legleu. Garamond was

... **lawyer,** continued

removed from the case after a prosecutor argued it was a conflict of interest for Garamond to lose a case and then argue his own incompetence on appeal.

Garamond complained that he had been defending 100 misdemeanor cases a week in Municipal Court.

He lodged his protest shortly after attorney James Hames withdrew from his contract as a public defender, saying he would have faced malpractice suits had he continued trying to defend so many clients. Hames said that he had been handling 1,100 to 1,200 cases a year—almost four times as many as permitted under guidlines established by the State Supreme Courtlast March.

"The system has broken down, and nobody much is trying to remedy it," Hames said.

Five days after Garamond decided not to defend Legleu, a new defender was assigned to assist Garamond in working with his caseload. Later, new defense attorneys were added to ease the caseloads in other divisions of Municipal Court.

Since then, Garamond has given up his contract to defend cases in Municipal Court.

"I'm sure I ruined a lot of relationships trying to fight the city of Brightsville," Garamond said.

Editing —Jet exercise

Edit this story as your instructor suggests.

MOSCOW (GLP)—The Soviet Union has recently displayed an array of aircraft

including its latest jet fighter, on Moscow TV in a way that might give the West a message.

The editor of *Jane's All the World's Aircraft* says he thinks Moscow is trying to tell the

West it is shedding its centuries-old mantel of secrecy.

Photos of the Sukhoi 27, a Mach-2.3 twin-engine jet praised as a counterpart of the U.S.

F-15 Eagle, have just been published in a new edition of *Jane's,* the leading aeronautic

reference work.

Editor John W.R. Taylor said the Soviets have superiority over the West in some kinds

of combat planes and that Soviet espionage "loads the dice heavily against the West."

He also said it was unusual for the Soviet public to be shown new military airraft. The

Soviets' other new fighters, the MiG-29 and MiG-31, have been in service for a year or

more but no photos of them have been made public in the West.

Taylor saidhis photos, taken from a TV screen, came from a Briton who had travelled

in Russia. He said he did not know when they were shown on television.

... jet, continued

Taylor said perhaps the photos "were put out as a softener," meant to show a move away from secrecy in case the incoming U.S. governmental leadership wants to respond.

The Sukhoi 27, which has the NATO code name "Flanker," is a twin-tailed jet with a profile similar to that of the F-15, which has been in service since the mid-1970s.

The Su-27 has "look down, shoot down" radar and armament which should give it "formidable potential against low-flying aircraft and cruise missiles," *Jane's* says.

Though the F-15 was long thought to be the world's best fighter, Assistant Secretary of Defense Donald Latham told *Janes* the MiG-31 is superior and that the Soviets "are producing it like gang-busters."

Taylor says in his foreword, "There was a time when the most advanced Soviet aircraft trailed far behind their Western counterparts. A glance through the Soviet section of this edition of *Jane's* will show how much the technology gap has narrowed."

He said a gigantic Soviet transport plane, the An-124 "Condor"; the Mi-28 attack helicopter; the heavy-lifting Mi-26 helicopter; and an air-to-air combat helicopter code-named "Hokum," in addition to the Su-27, of course, have helped the Soviets catch up.

... **jet,** continued

Taylor said the Soviets have made advances through their "the natural engineering

talent" and espionage. Stolen plans for the U.S. F-18 fightersaved the Soviets $55 million

and five years of development time, Taylor's publication says.

He noted that no reports of U.S. espionage successes ever come from the Soviet

Union, whose press does not cover such stories.

Editing —Indiafire exercise

Edit this as your instructor suggests.

NEW DELHI (GLP)—Flames and smoke killed at least 38 persons in a10-story luxury hotel before dawn today.

Officials said one American, was among the victims.

Some plunged to their deaths from the second and third flooors when they tried to escape the flames and smoke racing through the hotel, the Siddharth Continental Hotel.

It was the world's worst fire since 99 died in a New Year's Day blaze in Puerto Rico in 1987.

Amolng the injured was Christopher Roesel, 37, who works for the relief agency CARE in Thailand. He was recovering from smoke inhalation in a hospital. A spokesman for CARE in New York, Bill Dugan, said five other CARE employees escaped without injury.

At a press conference, authorities said 46 people were injured. Thirtyeight were hosptialized. Officials first thought 70 persons had been hurt.

Though no cause for the blaze was established, police and hotel personnel speculated an

. . . Indiafire, continued

electrtical short-circuit may have set a carpet afire in the Siddharth's ground-floor banquet

room.

Survivors said they never heard any alarm and that the staff and fire department were

poorly prepared for an evacuation.

"Nobody told us anything," said Phillipe Demerey, a businessman from Liege,

Belgium. "I looked out my window and saw the flames. I opened the door and the hall

was full of smoke. I left the hotel through the fire escape with only my nightclothes. I saw

people shouting for help. It was not very efficient the way they tried to help them."

Hosptial sources said the dead included about 20 foreigners, including three Britons,

two Japanese, two Australians, an Iraqi and at least one Soviet, plus, of course, the

American.

A U.S. Embassy official, speaking on the condition he not be identified, said the blaze

at the Siddharth killed one American. He declined to release the man's name pending

notification of next of kin, but hopsital sources identified the victim as Earl D. williams,

New York City.

Police said two diplomats, from West Germany and Argentina, also died. The United

. . . Indiafire, continued

News of India news agency said the victims included two infants.

Authorities are required by law to investigate the southern New Delhi hotel for possibly

causing death due to negligence.   No arrests have been made.

The hotel is owned by Siddharth Interncontinental Hotels Ltd. of India, and is not

affiliated with the Worldwide Intercontinental chain.

Police Commissioner Ved Marwah said "all aspects" of the fire would be investigated,

including arson.

The fire apparently began at 1:45 a.m. in the banquet room. Flames engulfed the first

three floors and sent thick smoke rolling upstairs, officials said.

"There was a stampede and all night people were running helter-skelter," one policeman

said, quoiting a victim. Officials said most of the dead suffocated or were killed by smoke

inhalation. "We found bodies on every floor," said a police officer who spoke on the

condition he not be identified. "Some of them were in their beds, others in the hallway."

A doctor at Safdarjang Hospital, where the injured and dead were taken, said at least

five people died of injuries suffered when they leaped out of windows on the hotel's

second and third floors.

... Indiafire, continued

Hotel staff members said the hotel was "practically full" with about 175 guests, about 40 percent of them foreigners.

George Allen, a businessman from Britain, said some guests tried to escape from the hotel blaze by tying sheets from their beds together and lowering themselves to safety.

"People were climbing down on sheets, but some of them caught fire. The fire brigade arrived, but there was no water in the tanks. It was 20 minutes before they started to do anything."

J.S. Malhotra, general manager of the hotel, was quoted by a news reporter as saying an alarm went off soon after employees in the cafeteria discovered the blaze. He was quoted as saying many guests did not hear the alarm because they were asleep.

Editing — Jobs exercise

Edit this story as your instructor directs.

Washington (GLP)—The federal government announced today a $95 million plan

to set up 32,000 new summer jobs in 31 cities across the United States.

The plan is meant to combat rising unemployment and unrest in urban areas,

White House spokesman Al Ameda said. It is aimed at the hard-core un-employed

especially youths and minorities. The program which requires no new approval from

congress, will use existing fedral manpower and job training agencies to screen and hire

applicants for positions in community srevice, propety managment and building

maintenance and repair.

The White house said also it has called for a speedup in the the spending of $250

million in already approved fedral public housing and health service projects to provide

5000 more jobs in the 31 selected cities.

The cities, are in 16 states and account for about 12 per cent of the U.S. population.

"We certainly realize," Ameda said, "95 million and 32,000 jobs are not enough to

alleviate the pain of the recession or to insure more rapidly economic recovery. But, at the

... jobs, continued

same time, because they are targeted to impact cities with the greatest need, cities where

poverty—with its resultant deleterious effects on our nations major asset, it's youth—we

expect that these programs we have funded from existing money and which we will put in

to operation immediately so that they will be impactful, timewise, will make a difference in

the quality of life in these cities.

Ameda pointed out that the jobs are in adition to the 1.4 millin jobs alredy

authorized under the fedral government's Summer Youth Employment Program.

Most of the news jobs will last from six to eight weeks, although some are expected

to continue into the fall.

The national unemployment rate soared to 9.7 per cent last month, the latest month

for which statistics are availbe for. But the rate soared further among teenaged youths, to

22.1 percent. In some large metropolises' inner-city areas the rate of enemployment is

even higher than that, and it has caused many leaders of urgan groups to warn of a "long,

hot summer" unless fedral govermental officials found ways to provide additional

employment assistance for those without jobs.

Editing — Houcrime exercise

Edit this story for a Texas newspaper in a city not on the list in the story. Prepare the questions you would ask if your city were on the list and you needed to improve the story.

Houston was the leading city in the state of Texas in the number of murders recorded

last year, according to FBI informatioin released this morning.

The information was put forth by the FBI in its quarterly Uniform Crime Reports,

which came out just before 9 a.m. The Report covered the period from January-December.

Houston was listed in first place in Texas and third in the nation in the number of

murders committeed with 716 murdered in the period covered by the FBI Report.

Dallas, with 505 murders listed on Bureau records, is listed in second place in the

report. Ft. Worth Was in third place with 319 murders, and San Antonio gunned into the

fourth slot with 199 corpses.

Nationwide, New York city was first in homicides with 1,299 slayings, followed by

Chicago, 999, Houston 617, Los Angeles, 644, Detroit, 640, and Philadelphia, Penna.,

sixth with 554.

Murders figures fo the 13 major texas cities of over 100,000 popplation, with last

... **Houcrime,** continued

year's homicide number followed by the comparable figure for the previous yuear:

Houston 716 and 698, Dallas 505 and 501, Fort Worth 318 and 277; San Antonio 199

and 187' Austin 74 and 75, Corpus Christ 34 and 24; Lubbock, 32 and 18; El Paso 28 and

27; Waco 27and seven. Beamont 251 and 21;Amarilo 11 and 10, Whichita Falls 9 and 7,

and Abilene six and 4.

Although the total number of Texans murdered was up by 99 from the previous

comparable tally of 2,978, thus breaking the 3,000 body barrier for the first time, Gov. Bill

Clements expressed guarded optimism. "We hjad a bad first quarter, losing nearly 900

Texans to killers, but things have settled down Obviously, we aren't perfect, but we are

trying to do better. I believe Texans will pull together and put a lid on this terrible thing for

the rest of the year and perhaps end the year under 3,000. Of course, we all hope we can

cut the figreu to zero someday so no Texan would endure the tragedy of an unnecessary

killing."

Editing — Oldcold exercise

Edit this as your instructor directs. Inasmuch as the story refers to cold weather, you need to know that today is the second Tuesday in February.

An 82-year-old Plaquemines County, La., woman who lay helpless in a gulley for two days apparently has survived her ordeal without harm.

Effie Staffan slipped into the ditch Satur;day afternoon and wasn't found tuntil 5 p.m. Monday. Even thjough the temperature dipped into the 30's during the two nights she was left in the cold wearing only a long frock and a sweater, brought, ironically, from Plaquemines, where it seldom gets cold, she was reported doing well this morning. Her daughter Bonnie Cody had one word to describe the events of the two day: "remarkable."

Mrs. Staffan was resting well at Memorial Hospital this morning. A spokesperson who gave out information to the press said she had been hospitalized for observation and is listed in satisfactory condition. Hopsital officials said they didn't know when the elderly lady would get out.

"She semed," said her daughter, "to be doing fine last night. She ate, and she hadn't had an;ything to eat in two days. However, Mrs. Cody said her mother is still

disoriented and thinks the entire two-day-long ordeal was just an unplesant dream.

Mrs. Cody, who grew up in White Castle, Louisiana, where Mrs. Staffen used to

live, said she learned her mother was missing at around 10 a.m. yesterday morning. ;

Neighbors called Mrs. Staffan to ask her to go shopping with them, and when she didn't

answer the telephone they became worried, said Mrs. Cody, who is 58 and talks with a

pronounced Cajon brogue. Neighbors then visited Mrs. Staffan's house, at 5703

Lakemoore and began caling relatives when they couldn't locate the old widow.

Mrs. Cody said she quickly notified the police and the search began.

About 40 rescue workers and policement searched the woods in the hills near Bull

Creek Park, in the far northwest part of the city, near loop 360 and rural route 2222.

"It was terrible," Mrs. Cody recalled. "I thought we would find her, but I didn't

think she'd be alive."

However, Mrs. Cody's fears vanished just before Dark. Heyward Neely, 68, a

retired carpenter who, ironically, once lived in Plaquemines Parish himself, found Mrs.

Staffan lying on her back in a steep, four-foot deep ditch.

"I found her laying on her back down there in that steep ditch," said Neely, who,

. . . oldcold, continued

with his wife, Elsie, 62, had decided to go for a walk in the countryside "during the cold

snap, which puts a sparkle into the woods" Neely said.

"It was just instinct or something," he said. Something just told me to go down in

there. I never did believe in miracles afore now," he said.

Mrs. Cody hsaid her mother had never wandered away from home before. ; "She

ain't senile, if that's what you mean, " Cody snapped at reporters. "She's got a good head

on her shoulders. I suspect she was just out walking for some exercise and fell into that

damned ditch. "I've told the county they ought fill it up, but they don't give a hoot about

us here."

"I regret that Mrs. Staffan fell in and sufered," said County Commissioner Bob

Fonts, in whose precinct the ditch lies, just across the city limits line, "but the county canot

fill in natural depressions that pose no general threat to well-being."

Mrs. Staffan's late husband, bert, died of exposure 11 years ago on a hunting trip

in Wyoming. He fell off a horse and received a broken leg. ; Searchers found his body

after three days in the wilderness, where temperatures got down to 40 degrees below zero.

Mrs. Staffan has two other daughters who make their residences here. They are

. . . oldcold, continued

Mrs. Earl Creech, 1105 Jackleg Lawyer lane, and Mrs. Anabess Hankamer, 202 Tyeutu

Terrace.

Mrs. Cody, who lives at 5411 Lakemoore Dr., said she has no idea how her mom

was able to survive the cold in the flimsy outfit wshe was wearing. ; But Cody, a divorcee,

said Mrs. Staffan "is a very strong-willed person. . . and she has always been extremely

healthy."

Mrs. Staffan dshad eatn her usual breakfast of yogurt and beet juice before setting

out on her walk. She suffered a little from dehydration, doctors informed

Editing — Jailtime exercise

Read this twice and understand it before you put a pencil to it. Then edit it as suggested by your instructor.

EL PASO (GLP)—Although Americans complain about being held without trial in drug cases in Mexico, Mexicans are often held in American jails for months without formal charges against them, sometimes even after they have completed sentences for illegal entry into the United States, Mexican officials say.

A Mexican government official says many consider the practice, legal under U.S. law, unfair and discriminatory to Mexicans.

The Mexican aliens are held in the United States under bonds as material witnesses in alien smuggling cases, assistant U.S. Attorney Greg Miller said.

But Americans who are material witnesses in such cases are almost never required to post bond and are released on their personal recognizance, he said.

Miller said the average number of Mexicans held as material witnesess at any time in San Antonio is usually 12 to 15. Holding aliens as material witnesses is not uncommon along the border, he said.

The Mexican consul-general in San Antonio, Raul Gonzales-Garces, has criticized

. . . **jailtime,** continued

the policy, which he says is applied in a discriminatory fashion to Mexican citizens.

Gonzales-Garces said that Americans often complain about being held in Mexican

jails for months and months without bond while they await judicial resolution of drug-

related charges. But he said the same treatment applies equally to Mexican citizens who

also spend months in jail without bond in similar cases. "That is our law," he said.

Gonzales-Garces said Mexicans jailed in the United States can seldom post the

bond--usually $5,000 to $10,000--because they have no money. "They came here looking

for work," he said.

Miller said the procedure is used to hold the Mexicans as witnesses in alien-

smuggling cases because, if released, they probably would not be available for trials

against the smugglers. He said they are held on complaints signed by the U.S. Attorney's

office.

"Their testimony is crucial in making cases on these smuggling rings, Miller said.

Mexican witnesses are held in the El Paso County jail under contract with the

federal govenrment. They are paid $6 a day, a fee which Gonzalez-Garces called "totally

humiliating."

... jailtime, continued

"We make a concerted effort not to keep anyone in custody for more than 45 to 60

days," Miller said.

In most of the cases, Miller said, the aliens are not prosecuted or sentenced for

illegal entry inth tothe United States.

The jail time served by the aliens as material witnesses usually in not longer than

they would spend if sentenced for illegal entry, Millar said. In a few cases, some aliens are

detained as material wetnesses even after completing sentences for illegal entry, he said.

About 800,000 Mexican aliens are deported from the United States each year, and

Miller said only about 5 per cent of them are ever tried for illegal entry.

"We tried releaseing them (the Mexican witnesses) on personal recognizance bonds,

but they would just head north or back across the border," he said.

"We had one case where we released 13 witnesses. When the trial came up, all 13

had disappeared."

Under U.S. law, Miller said, a person is entitled to confront witnesses in a trial.

An assistant U.S. attorney in Los Angeles said that as many as 80 Mexican aliens

. . . jailtime, continued

have been held at one time in the Los Angeles County jail as material wtitnesses.

The Los Angeles federal lawyer said many o the Mexican witnesses had

disappeared before trials when they were released.

Gonzales-Garces said he is not bitter about the Mexicans held as material witnesses.

It is a legal procedure in the United Staes, he said. But he said Americans should be more

understanding of the Mexican law when Americans are not allowed to post bond in drug

cases and are jailed during long judicial proceedings. "We have found that our proceedings

are really, the only way to fight the illicit traffic of drugs," he said.

Editing — Chase exercise

Edit this story as your instructor suggests.

A Michigan man was killed yesterday when he crashed his stolen car into a tree on Nevada-Wynford Rd. following a high-speed chase with law enforcement officers from two counties.

The victim was identified this morning as Russell T. Faulkner, 23, a car salesman from Milford. He was taken to Memorial Hospital by Bryd Ambulance and was declared dead there by County Coroner Steven Kim, who ruled that death was caused by massive chest injuiries and internal bleeding.

Faulkner was carrying no identification at the time of the accident; however, identification belonging to a woman was found in the car.

Deputy Sheriff Ron Shawber said Friday night the victim may have been man wanted by Michigan authorities as a suspect in the theft of the car, a 1987 black Corvette, reported stolen from a Rochester Hills, Mich. (Detroit area) car dealer. It is not known if the car Faulkner worked for the dealership where the car, valued at $29,000, was stolen.

Faulkner's body was taken from the hospital to Wise Funeral Home later in the evening. Services and burial will be held in Milford.

... **chase,** continued

Units from the Brightsville andMarion Highway Patrol posts, the Central and Travis

County Sheriff's Offices, Brightsville and Wynford police departments were all involved in

the chase, which officials say reached speeds of well over 100 miles per hour.

According to Patrol spokesman Sgt. Ernest Howard, the chase began about 5:18 p.m.

on State Hwy. 23 in Travis County. A trooper on patrol ran a routine check on the

vehicle's Michigan dealer's plates through the national computer which revealed that the car

was stolen.

The car was stopped on State 67; however, Faulkner sped off at a high rate of speed as

the trooper started to exit his cruiser.

Troopers in twowo Patrol cars spotted the fleeing vehicle and pursued it west on State

67, but they lost sight of the car after about six or seven miles because of the high speeds.

Sheriff's Department reports say deputies spotted the car headed east on U.S. 30 about

5:35. Deputies chased the car east on the bypass when Faulkner turned around and was

pursued west by two sheriff's cars, two Patrol cars and a Brightsville police car.

All five units lost sight of the car as speeds reached in excess of 115 miles per hour.

Travis County deputies set up a roadblock at the intersection of U.S. 30 and Farm Road

... **chase,** continued

231 while Faulkner was spotted headed south on the county line by a Highway Patrol

aircraft which had been working in the County all day.

A Central County sheriff's deputy picked up the chase at that point and pursued the

vehicle, which was next seen headed east on Nevada-Wynford Rd.

Meanwhile, another deputy spotted the car again at the intersection of of County Line

Rd. and attempted to slow the vehicle. The deputy said Faulkner slowed to about five

miles per hour before passing in front of the cruiser and accellerating.

The deputy once again took up the chase east on Nevada-Wynford Rd. when Faullkner

suddenly veered left of center on a straight stretch of highway and rammed into a mMaple

tree in the front lawn of a home owned by Dale Heistand, 552 Nevade-Wynford Rd.

Heistand, who witnessed the crash, said he was listening to the chase on a scanner and

stepped out on his porch when he heard sirens moments before the crash.

He told this reporter that it appeared Faulkner struck the tree deliberatey. His home is

four-tenths of a mile east of Marion-Melmore Rd.

"I seen him turn his steerin' wheel when he come to this here (north) side of the road,"

. . . **chase,** continued

Heistand said. "I thokught there was something in the road. I looked back and there was nothing coming.

"Just about the time I turnt back, (the car) hit my dang tree. I ducked and the next thing I saw was all the (debris) blowing (east)."

The coronor was not available for comment about the reason for the crash.

The crash occurred about 5:30 and Faulkner was freed from the wreckage about 40 minutes later by rescuers using the Jaws of Life tool and pry bars.

Deputies estimate the car was traveling in excess of 95 miles per hour and debris was scattered as far as 700 feet from the crash site. There were no skid marks.

The front end of the car was destroyed and the engine shoved into the driver's compartment, pinning the driver underneath. One of the front wheels of the vehicle was found in a wheat field about 200 yards from the tree.

Several trucks from the Wynford Volunteer Fire Department stood by in case of fire although the rear portion of the car managed to stay relatively intact. The wreck was towed away on a flat bed truck from Carl Massey's Wrecking Service.

The fatality is the fifth violent death to occur in the county this year.

Headlines

Your name _____

Date _____

Headlines — Exercise 1

You do not need lengthy instructions on this part; you have had expert guidance from your instructor and a wonderful chapter in your textbook. Put that to good use. Some good headline writers like to write more than one kind of headline on a story, in addition to the assigned version. That is, they might do a two-line head after doing the required one-liner. Or they might try to say the same thing in fewer words. Any such effort—it's sort of like batting practice—will pay off for you. You are likely to write headlines in any kind of job except pure reporting—and the discipline involved in word play will help you even there.

Write a one-line headline with a count of 35-38.

_____

SAN ANTONIO—It may look like a muddy war zone, but it is just the littered bottom of the downtown San Antonio River—drained of water and visible to all.

And Ron Darner, the city's Parks and Recreation Department director, does not like it any more than do visitors who are enticed to stroll the channel after hearing about the romantic River Walk.

"The river was drained because of damage to the retaining wall," Darner said Monday. "Once that's repaired, we'll fill it again and restore the beauty of this place."

Write a one-line headline with a count of 30-32

_____

WASHINGTON—A House subcommittee has approved $10 million for the next fiscal year to begin building an Army Medical Center in Brightsville, despite a recent Pentagon decision overturning plans to build a 450-bed replacement for the hospital.

The center's supporters hope the vote is the first step in having Congress reverse the Pentagon proposal, which would kill the replacement hospital and build instead a 150-bed facility while combining operations with Wilford Hall Air Force Medical Center.

. . . exercise 1, continued

Write a one-line headline with a count of 26-28.

_____

Brightsville appears to be the heart transplant center of the nation this week. Two heart transplants have been performed locally, a third Brightsvillite is recovering after undergoing the procedure in Virginia, and a fourth is awaiting the operation in California.

Doctors involved with the transplants believe the sudden surge in the procedures reflects the recent availability of the transplants and a backlog of patients awaiting hearts—along with a good measure of coincidence and luck.

Write a one-line headline with a count of 29-33.

_____

Members of the Brightsville Lake Board agreed today on the need to better protect a remote lake location that has been the site of a violent crime rampage.

The board proposed locking gates to the isolated Middle River Park, increasing patrols and lighting the camping areas, the site of two major crimes in the past week.

Write a two-line headline, with lines of 22-24 counts each.

_____

_____

WASHINGTON—The secretary of state said today a congressional report alleging widespread misuse of U.S. aid to anticommunist rebels was a politically motivated effort to discredit the administration's Central America policy.

"I think the track record on the funds we have had available is basically excellent," the secretary said. He spoke in response to a General Accounting Office report that millions of dollars in aid has been diverted to private use.

. . .exercise 1, continued

Write a two-line headline of 20-23 counts per line on the story about the parrot. We will do two headlines on this story. Let's assume, after you complete the first headline, that the person who assigns headlines has a change of mind and wants something else on the story. That will take you to the second headline.

_____

_____

All right, now try the same story with three lines and 15-17 counts per line. You may use some or all of the original headline's wording, but you are not required to; we threw that one away.

_____

_____

_____

A black woman in Brightsville has filed a harassment complaint against a white neighbor who, the black woman charges, has trained a parrot to squawk a racial slur.

The woman, Charlene Tymony, said her neighbor trained the parrot to speak the offensive word because of a dispute that began when Tymony refused to trim her trees to improve the neighbor's view.

Detectives will investigate the complaint, but a police spokesman said he was uncertain whether the city's harassment law covers animals.

Write a two-line headline with lines of 17-19 each.

_____

_____

. DALLAS—The petroleum industry's recession has brought hard times to charities, many of which are cutting budgets and looking for ways to spread their diminished funds across increased needs.

The drop in Houston, for example, is being felt sharply by United Way. The organization expects a $3.2 million shortage in its funding projections for about 80 charitable agencies in the area.

Your name _____

Date _____

Headlines —Exercise 2

Write a two-line headline with lines of 17-19 each.

_____

_____

WASHINGTON—The U.S. government has told former President Ferdinand Marcos that continued meddling in Philippine politics could jeopardize his status as a political exile in the United States.

Administration officials said Marcos, who has been in Hawaii since he was deposed, was told as recently as two weeks ago that partisan political activity "is not consistent with his status as a guest of this country."

Write a three-line headline with lines of 12-15 each.

_____

_____

_____

NEW YORK—Thousands of demonstrators filled Central Park today, singing, chanting and carrying signs opposing South African racial policy. They demanded that the president impose rigid economic sanctions.

"We must remove our ambassador and stop Americans from doing business in South Africa, as we've done already in Libya," said Arthur Ashe, a former professional tennis player. "We must put our moral weight on the side of the people in South Africa, fighting for freedom.

. . . exercise 2, continued

Write a two-line headline with lines of 23-25 each.

_____

_____

Brightsville's latest brush with disaster came to an end at 6 p.m. yesterday—six days after chemical tankers from a Middle Pacific train derailed and exploded, forcing 750 residents from their homes.

Evacuees began returning to their homes as soon as the police barricades came down. Emergency crews working nonstop had removed the danger of a explosion from tankers among the twisted wreckage of the fatal train wreck.

Write a three-line headline with lines of 14-16 each. This story follows the one above by one day.

_____

_____

_____

A smoldering fire in a covered grain car was doused yesterday afternoon to prevent an explosion at the Middle Pacific Railroad derailment site, where a week earlier a chemical spill produced gas that chased hundreds from their homes.

The burning grain car, which had been smodlering since the dertailment, could have exploded if oxygen had mixed with the grain dust, said District Fire Chief Alfred Sandoval.

Headlines — Exercise 3

Write a one-line headline of 40-44 counts.

_____

If you have ever passed a group of footbag players with a barely suppressed longing to rush in and kick the thing to kingdom come, stay away from Brightsville City Park from noon to 5 p.m. Saturday. During those hours, the third annual Brightsville Hacky Sack Festival converges on the park's Frisbee Golf course.

Write a one-line headline of 25-27 counts, and a kicker of the same count. (As you recall, the kicker, being in smaller type, will not take up as much space.)

(Kicker here) _____

(Main line) _____

It's enough to break a guitar player's heart: Walk into some of the city's most popular clubs, and instead of a four-piece rock band tucked into the corner you will find a video monitor.

Video has not quite killed the radio star, but it certainly has been a knife in the back of the stage-struck kid with the cheap guitar and big dreams. Ditto for the booking agent, the guy the kid hires to find places to play.

"A couple of years ago we had a real strong live music scene, says John Ertl, who at age 28 is already a knowledgeable veteran of Brightsville booking work. "Even though the music was stylistically behind the East and West coasts, the public didn't know it was. Now, with MTV, they can see national acts in their living rooms. And the baby boomers are staying home with the kids."

. . . exercise 3, continued

Write a three-line headline of 15-17 counts per line.

＿＿＿＿＿＿＿＿＿＿＿＿＿＿＿＿＿＿＿＿

＿＿＿＿＿＿＿＿＿＿＿＿＿＿＿＿＿＿＿＿

＿＿＿＿＿＿＿＿＿＿＿＿＿＿＿＿＿＿＿＿

The trial of two men accused of tampering with the Central County government telephone system so they could prove their phone-tapping theory has been postponed to next month.

The case, which first entered the courts two years ago, also has been assigned to a new judge and prosecutor. County Superior Court Judge Michael Irwin took the case after other judges disqualified themselves a week ago.

Write a two-line headline of 24-27 counts per line.

＿＿＿＿＿＿＿＿＿＿＿＿＿＿＿＿＿＿＿＿＿＿＿＿＿＿

＿＿＿＿＿＿＿＿＿＿＿＿＿＿＿＿＿＿＿＿＿＿＿＿＿＿

Brightsville police and school officials deny claims by a California group that a proposed child molestation prevention program "would rip apart innocent families."

Police, school district officials and school board members have scheduled another presentation on the proposed program for 7 p.m. Monday at Groves Elementary School. The presentation was set up to give parents another chance to hear about the proposal, to voice concerns and to ask questions, Superintendent Pat Carlin said.

Board members are scheduled to vote Wednesday on whether to implement the program, which police officers say would be geared toward preventing the abuse of young children.

. . . exercise 3, continued

Write a headline of three lines, with a count of 15-18 on each line.

_____

_____

_____

NEW ORLEANS—At least two automobiles fell from the Lake Pontchartrain Bridge today after a freighter hit a support and left a 40-foot gap in the road high above the lake.

Four people are thought to have died in the two cars.

Divers have been called and will try to find the victims. The water is about 250 feet deep where the accident occurred.

Write a headline of three lines, with a count of 15-18.

_____

_____

_____

ATLANTA—Saying he was fed up with the job, an Elred Airlines pilot climbed out of his jetliner while awaiting takeoff clearance today. He left 83 stunned passengers sitting in the plane.

Angered by a problem with a galley door, a fuel shortage and a projected 20-minute wait before taxiing, the pilot simply left the plane. The flight, to Tampa, was delayed two hours before another pilot was found.

"I'm fed up with this stuff. I'm sick and tired of the treatment. I'm hanging it up. You can have it. This was my last flight," the departing pilot said to the passengers.

... **exercise 3,** continued

Write a three-line headline with 10-12 counts per line.

_____

_____

_____

A minority-run firm hired by the city's Housing Authority to manage the $5 million remodeling of the Village Housing Project was fired yesterday, after the authority's assistant secretary locked the firm's employees out of the project's offices.

Officials of the company, Deiter Engineering, of Valdosta, Ga., immediately contended that the authority discriminated against the firm. They said they would file a lawsuit in Federal Court to force the authority to pay the company.

Write a two-line headline of 20-22 counts per line.

_____

_____

WASHINGTON—Wholesale gasoline prices ended a four-month tumble and rose .06 percent last month, the Labor Department reported this morning.

Despite the increase, the department said producer prices for the past six months had declined at an annual rate of 7.6 percent. That is the steepest overall six-month decline since the government began keeping track of wholesale prices in 1947.

Headlines — Exercise 4

Write a lively one-line headline of 34-37 counts.

_____

DENVER—Under a bright sun and with a breeze that snapped hundreds of banners, the crowds roared.

More than a decade after the war in Vietnam ended, Coloradoans paused to thank the men and women who risked their lives in that unpopular war.

In a homecoming parade organized by friends and relatives of veterans, thousands marched through the streets to Mile-High Stadium, where they received the city's plaudits from state and local officials.

Write a two-line headline of 30-32 counts per line.

_____

_____

ATLANTA—The Rev. Adrian Rogers, newly elected fundamentalist president of the Southern Baptist Convention, told delegates yesterday that he rejects the "monkey mythology" of evolution and "wouldn't give half a hallelujah" for the heavenly chances of anyone who doubts the virgin birth.

Rogers, who was supported by the denomination's strict fundamentalist wing in Tuesday's election, assailed religious liberalism and praised "the conservative gospel" to delegates at the Georgia World Congress Center.

Your name _____

Date _____

... **exercise 4,** continued

Write a four-line headline—yes, a four liner—with a maximum count of 12 per line.

_____

_____

_____

_____

Bright skies and brisk sales brought smiles to artists' faces and dollars to their pocketbooks yesterday as the 12th annual Festival of Arts began on the grounds of the Brightsville Art Museum.

Forecasts of scattered thundershowers did not bother eager sellers or amenable buyers. Two hundred exhibitors—131 of them from out of state—opened their booths to surprisingly good business.

Write a two-line headline with lines of 23-25 counts.

_____

_____

CHICAGO—A doctor who used a herbicide to treat obesity at three clinics in the Midwest faces a $100,000 fine because of allegations by the Illinois state's attorney that he violated a court order prohibiting use of the herbicide.

State District Judge Daren Hollman Jr. ordered a hearing for Dr. Nick Brahmsinsky after a hearing today in which the state's attorney accused employees of Brahmsinsky's Chicago clinic of continuing to praise the herbicide's effectiveness in weight-loss treatment.

... exercise 4, continued

Write a three-line headline with lines of 13-16.

_____

_____

_____

A 25-year-old mother managed to save two of her children from a raging motel fire, but her 7-month old baby died in the flames.

Authorities said the mother, Cynthia Longoria, ran back into the smoke-filled room to look for the baby, Stacy, but she collapsed. Fire fighters dragged her to safety but did not find the baby in time to save it.

Write a two-line headline with lines of 23-25 counts.

_____

_____

LOUDON, N.H.—At least four people died in motorcycle accidents and more than 200 were arrested yesterday as thousands of bikers packed into New Hampshire for the nation's oldest motorcycle race.

The 64th annual Kawasaki Loudon Classic, which once sparked bloody riots, saw arrests only for minor offenses, police said.

Write a one-line headline with a maximum count of 38.

_____

EDMONTON, Alberta—The operators of an indoor mall where a roller coaster accident killed three people said today all rides will remain closed for a week-long investigation.

A company statement on the Saturday night accident of the Mindbender ride, billed as the world's largest indoor roller coaster, said the track and cars will be examined "inch by inch." A switching failure has been tentatively blamed for the accident.

Headlines — Exercise 5

Write a three-line headline of 15-18 counts per line.

_____

_____

_____

MANILA—Nine thousand impoverished Filipinos elbowed their way through the opulent palace of the deposed ruler Ferdinand Marcos today on the anniversary of his departure. President Corazon Aquino publicly criticized his selfish extravagance in a speech to the throng.

So tremendous was the turnout that Aquino issued a midafternoon appeal for a more orderly tour of the Spanish colonial mansion, which Marcos barred to the public until his 20-year reign ended.

Write a three-line headline with lines of 14-16 counts each.

_____

_____

_____

Daniel Walker's $2 million civil suit against Megastate University and four present and past trustees could go to a County Superior Court jury today.

Testimony in the trial of the suit ended yesterday. The last codefendant to testify said that when he worked on a buy-out of Walker's contract he did not know Walker was about to be indicted on embezzlement charges.

. . . **exercise 5,** continued

Write a one-line headline of 20-23 counts on the Las Vegas story below.

_____

Inasmuch as the story has some oddity to it, let's do another headline. Try a three-liner of up to 15 counts per line. You should be able to tell more about the crash this time.

_____

_____

_____

LAS VEGAS—A helicopter and a twin-engine plane, both carrying sightseers, collided at 8,000 feet and crashed in flames into the Grand Canyon today, killing all 25 aboard.

Coconino County sheriff's officers reported 20 dead in the plane, which was carrying foreign tourists, and five dead in the helicopter. The plane had a crew of two; the helicopter carried four passengers and the pilot.

Write a one liner of 39-42 counts.

_____

MCALLEN, Texas—A coalition endorsing undocumented workers' rights announced today it supports Border Patrol objections to private vigilante groups like the Ku Klux Klan that attempt to enforce immigration law.

The announcement followed a meeting by coalition members with Silvestre Reyes, McAllen Border Patrol chief, concerning the recent KKK visit to Border Patrol headquarters.

... **exercise 5,** continued

OK, here's a toughie to end the book. Give us a three-line headline with lines counting 17-19 each. Go out with a flair. If you prefer, set the book on fire and go out with a flare.

_____

_____

_____

LAKE HAVASU CITY, Ariz.—A combination astronomical observatory and resort is being proposed for the Hualapai Mountains, 30 miles south of Lake Havasu City.

A Phoenix partnership told the Mohave County Board of Supervisors Monday that it hopes to buy or lease land from the state or federal governments for the $40 million project. The commercial observatory and 200-bed resort would be near Granite Peak, which stands 7,069 feet high at the southern end of the mountain range. The proposed name of the facility is the Observation Point.

Brightsville City Directory

All entries in this directory are correct.

A

Apson Betty dir MU Rec Spts, 2992 17th St

Armstrong Anthony carpenter 210 E 9th St

Avedon Carl (Ismelda) owner Rainbow restr 1212 S. Congress

Azle Alex (Letitia, clk Wolfe Nursery) const 99 Sixth

B

Botha Rolly (Beatrice) mgr Afro American Frndshp House, 1211 Brown Ct

Byroads Les exec State Republican Party 2222 Steck Av

Barnnock Michael (Nancy tchr Barton Elem) Barnnock Ins, 5561 Lamar

Batcock Les (Diana) dent 1331 Weltlich Apt 6A

Baulo Manfred (Maggie rptr Third Coast) owner Nickypicky, 344 Long Dr

Bayles Paul (Cathy asst pstr First Baptist) atty 4 Deep Elm

Biafracisco Quentin (Flagelita) med tech Memorial Hosp1433 Rincon St

Begum Bartholemew (Bea) baker, BBB Buns, 5699 Kingman

Bigelow Frank ownr Hathaway Carpets 7765 Kinsolving

Blakenship Frank (Flo watrs Ellis's rest) repr Sears 6388 Picapole Rd

Bliss Hardwinter (Chapita) secy Southland Corp 2355 Jeffrey Ln

Bodie Mary Jane PR Memorial Hospital 3030 Gunsight Terr

Boggs Tommy (Susie treas Watkins, Glenn) slsm Southland Corp 217 Roe St

Boggsy Bugakar (Betsy) pres Hurley Corp 7004 Caulla Dr

Bond James (Abundatora, model) author 007 M St

Bouldin Brent night mgr Cross Country Inn 2380 Del Curton

Bowie David celebrity 2001 E 42nd St

Bramer Bill (Carole, mgr Conway Pizza) 2814 Amore Blvd

Brandon William (Edora, tchr) prin Shiner Elem 6869 Running Rope Cove

Brensk Rosemary phys Memorial Hospital 3233 Statesman Cir

Brophy Candace (wid Earl) hairdrsr 4598 Sandestin Ct

Brooks Robert (Gloria, sec MU) dent 4576 Pullem Av

Brownard Billy Bob (Ester, watrs) slsm 1996 Nightclub Ln

Browning Hap (Alice atty) ptr,1938 Mercedes

Bruce Robert studt MU 12222 Farm Rd 111

Bryan Bob (Lallia, nurse Memorial) dpty sheriff 9012 Brightwood Terr

Burchette Margaret tchr Brightsville HS 3776 Nattydress Blvd

Burns Herman (Sally phy) tennis pro 4040 Deuce Terr

Burris Jack (Midle mech) dr W.W. Black Lines 878 Flakes Av

Butler Fidel (Collene ofc mgr) cstdn Interfirst Bank 28, 814 S Branch Av

C

Capps Ken (Sue) pharm 3499 Vincent

Castello joseph priest St. Elmo's Episcopalian 2323 Gudentensions Rd

Carisle Ross (Rosy univ prof) univ prof 8312 Gestalt Rd

Carlisle Wilhelm (Trudy) pres Carlisle mfg 1984 Orwell Rd

Carlson Don (Maybeth editor) research supvr Raymar 22 Foli St

Carnarski Pietr (Rusla) vet 2570 Lhasa Apsa Av

Carriion James mgr Blue's Mkt 2980 Thumbscale Way

Carzok Ruth wid 4532 rep Surety secy 8928 Maidenform Bra

Castinette Clacky (Sandra tech phy ofc) Army lt Schoffield Barracks.

Castings L.A. (Bernel pers wkr Raytheon 1213 Cat Mountain Dr

Caszalas Ken (Ruby) bartender Scribblers' 3030 Alshirote

Cesar Ron critic 2501 Guadalupe

Charise Cherry waitress 1801D Manor Downs Rd

Cheyney Wesley (Marilyn phy) 4741 Nye Rd

Cheyvalone Martin (Anne) mgr Harpoon Henry's 5558 IH35, # 44

Clapper Harold (Virginia) owner The Art Gallery 2001Beesi Ln

Cody Bonnie (Ledbetter, owner Cody's Gulf) mech White Auto 23 24th St

Cohan James (Sybil) tech, Computerland 7787 Atlantic Blvd

Cohen Ross (Sybil) asst mgr Brightsville National Bank 3400 Wayward Ln

Coldfarb Sweeny (Priscilla) state rep 1185 N Highland Av

Cortez Hernando exec Brigahtsville Explorer posts Faraway Pl

Course Alphred (Nancie) supm clk 4333 Safeway Dr

Creech Earl (Annette) atty 1105 Jackleg Lawyer Ct

Crinoline Fred (Suzanne) clothing mfg exec 9 Rodale Rd

Cuellar Elisando (Maria cook Tres Amigos) mgr Tres Amigos 12 Acton Rd

D

Dacron Debbie nurse3009 Galston La #3

Davies N.G. (Edith) asst cty atty 3493 Elm Ter

Davis Robert (Kelley TV anchor) dir city utilities 2824 Envoy Ln

Dawson Isador (Alicia) 844 Luxor Ln

Deutch John city cnclmn 5602 Claydesta Blvd

Dickinson Farleigh (Bess) professor, 333 Pretentious Pl

Downs Shirley, ret libn, 3098 Red Bud Tr

Dupre Leon L (Neva) clk, Safeway 22 Redbud Rd

E

Elred Betty psyclgst 1204 N Main St

Elred Martin (Nancy) professor MU, 5603 Lakemoore

Ernste Ralph (Rowena) ret 1207 Elm Terr

F

Fields Leo (Jo) ownr Downtown Western Wear 1365 Kilo St

Figueres Manny (Rita) city cnclmn, plmbr 884 Colquitt St

Flawn J Vernon (Lucille dispr Becker Trucking Co) truck dr 827 Pigeon Rd

Flowers Alfred (Tradusora) city cncilman 4700 Eastland Blvd

Fray Dave (Ellen tchr) coach Col Crawford HS, 4590 Chewbacca Rd

Friendly Daniel exec dir Community Action Center 853 Bellmont Av

G

Garamond Herb (Claire) atty 1998 Wuncall St

Gibson, Martin L. Red (Nancy) , leg puller, 5603 Lakemoore Dr

Glick Miriam (Pete, painter) exec

Central County 2576 Lungrattle Dr

Gordon Donnel taxi drvr 2000 W 12th St

Graham Howell (Eretria) dvlpr 8933 La Cienaga

Graham Ross R (Estella cty com) phys 710 Harding Av

Greenspan Art wid Charlene retd Manor Rd

Grindstone John J (Betty) exec IBM, 3569 Cat Mountain Ln

Gutenberg Sean (Isolde) cobbler 5501-D Shoofly Av.

H

Hames James (Turlock pastor 1st Baptist) atty 4646 Jaycock Blvd

Hankamer Everett (Anabess) trck drvr Union City Transfer 202 Tyeutu Terr

Heinz Rudy (Gloria tchr) Superior Court jdge 1120 Hardway Rd

Heistadt Dale (Saradora) farmer 552 Nevada-Wynford Rd

Himmelblau Betty (Ralph piano tuner) jeweler3443 Moonlight Dr

Holt Benjamin (Daisy cashier Goodwill Industries) bus drvr 5580 19th St

Honts Bob (Beth) cnty cmsr 8283 Blessed Way

Howard Ernest (Mary, tchr) Highway Patrol sgt 4322 Squibb's Crossing Ct

I

Ibolla Yassir eng Cummings Corp. 788 Pierre Blvd

Isaccs Marylu (Gary pilot) exec Beatrice 3788 Tuckaway Cove Corner

J

James Bob (Letitia) cty cnclmn 6787 Ranchero Av

Jansch Ernst R (Jill insptr Holten

Mfg) asmblr Holten Mfg 7403 Foxboro Dr

Janos Enos (Osiris tchr Hustings Elem) tchr Hustings elem 1877 Harnessbell Ln

Jernigan Cindy rptr Third Coast 5050 Division

Jones Jesse (Myra) pastor Holiness Pres 4 E Riverside Dr

K

Kesyl Dave (Lucille, clrk J.C. Penney) police sgt, 8777 Guadalupe

Kim Steven (Aphra) cnty coroner 8003 Awello Av

Knotte Otto (Gretchen owner Old Heidelberg rstnt) city sewer eng, 1999 Eggshell Terr

Knowe Martin (Donna teacher) ptlmn, 1998 Gayferd Rd

Koonce Earl (Ardyce, tchr) soc wkr 1177 Kennedy Ln

Koonce Gearl (Kathy, tchr) oil driller 2221 Midland St

L

Leglue Lydia clk Piggly Wiggly 5843 Rosemary Dr

Leigh Vivvy N actrs 1865 Mitchell St

Lhasa Lisa clk govnr ofc 1704 W Onslaw St

Long L. Dupre (Neva tchr BISD) gentleman sailor, 4308 Yellow Rose Tr

Lyrer Philip (Una) clk Holiday Inn 165 W Wensly

M

Mabry Ann wid Doc auditor Holiday Inn 1801 W 35th St

Maldonado Jose (Maria) farm wrkr 32333 Salver Tr

Marshal Bailey (Becky) dir HS Ath League, 2207 Shiloh Dr

Martin Raymond (Priscilla artist) clk Holiday Inn 77 Sunset St

Massey Carl (Gloria) ownr wrecking

svc 3398 Junkyard Dog St

McCarthy K.L. (Amy) supt cnty roads 8793 Pothole Ln

McClain Bobby (Hilo) ownr McClain Eng. 334 Postal Rd.

McDee Mike (Anne) mayor Gracie Mansion

Milloy John (Mildred mgr doughnut store) dvlpr 7343 Coonskin St

Moore Burnes G dir personnel school dist 8009 Diadem Cir

Muffeay Megan TV rptr 22 Harcourt St

Murray Blair (Patricia) mgr Beneficial Finance 1748 N 3rd St

N

Neeley B.W. owner Neeley's Grill 7763 Old Dutchman Rd

Neely Heyward (Elsie) retd 4556 Ladera Norte Tr

Newell Don (Faella) mgr Holiday Inn South 2200 I-35.

O

Obermark Jerome jdge 223 Judicial Rd

Ohaire, Madylyn palm rdr 4599 Billiegraham Av

O'Keefe Earl (Lou) ownr Hidden Bayou Apts 988 Bayou Terr

Osborn Erwin (Joan) phys 813 Alton Rd

Osburne, Burl (Lydia) supt. BISD, 20 Upping St

Owens Mary Sharpe (Melvin, dr) asst supt BISD 5888 Tunafish Ct

P

Pantera Paul (Allison secy BISD) mech Covert Buick 449 Revemup Tr

Paloma LA (Francene) diver Searama 2200 Doll Fin Rd

Pat Pitty baby berther 191 GWTW Rd

Plumley William (Leann dsptchr cnty

sheriff) sheriff dpty 338 Huntem Av

Q

Quick Sewte 121 Windmill way

Quinn, John M (Kathy) assoc. dean MU Com, 8721 Silverhill Ln

R

Ralfernst E.R. (wid Naomi) retd 204 Long Av

Ralph Ernst musician 7021 Mel Dr

Randall Gregg race drvr 3099 Diogenes St

Redford Emmett S (Nina) VP HS Ath Lge 6967 Vallejo Rd

Renfro Mike (Una) cnty jdg

Rountree Roger (Lavis) detective cty 135 Cuffim St

S

Scott Alan (Sybil) retd 2222 Rockwood Ln

Shawber Ronald (Nancy) dpty sheriff 7479 Bukim Rd

Singer S. Griffin (Evelyn) jnlsm prof MU 8113 Greenslope Dr

Sloan Roland (Margaret atty) municipal jdge 2989 Margo Rd

Smith Santone taxi drvr 2004 W 12th St

Staffan Effie retd 5411 Lakemoore

Staykempt Tom state's atty 2919 Harlandale

T

Timmons Vallejo (Betty Mae Odell) veg frmr 29999 Rutabaga Ln

Tittle Mel (Lou atty) city editor Gazette 1186 Hahtonna Tr

Tizzard, Lewis (Marie) slsmn Rentco 4877 Hannah Av

Thomas Gerald studt 981 Kasper Av

Thompson Alvarez (Betsi) police sgt

U

Ubberoth Pietro (Mame singer Torch Club) mgr Metro Opera 11008 Hycee Ct

Unan Dinasti (Lilli) cook Jack-in-the-Box 2874 Grecibuns Av

V

Valdez Montego (Sue mgr coffee shop) retd 418 E Graves St

Verth Alfred (Carla airline stwrds) travel agt 3998 Lakemoore Dr

W

Washburn Cary (Lynnette taxi dsptchr Yellow) mgr K-Mart 33 18th St

Williams Pat (Earl retd) cnty exec 2215 Hwy 12

Willianosski Fredreich (Eubella maid) cstdl engr MSU 3457 Yakima Rd

Willis Levi (Claudia, ownr KLBH-TV) cook McDonald's 1313 Niles Pl

Winslow Don (Nancy) Navy pilot retd, 4555 Calamari St

Wohlmann Gotfried mgr White's Auto 4768 Springhill Rd

Wounds, Guttschott (Denise, fashion designer) trapper, 1213 Possum Hollow

Wright Arthur (Lilli, stock brkr) 3989 Lakewood Blvd # 4

Wright Rollie (Evelyn, tchr) stock brkr 3989 Lakewood Blvd # 3

Y

Yelberton Abraham (Tittle, actrs) retd 2998 Easy Living Ln

Z

Zumwalt, Elmo (Mannie) retd mil, 2231 Sixth St.